Twe
and Happy

*A complete guide to happiness
in a little pocketbook*

By Pavie Valsa

Twenties and Happy

Copyright © 2019: Pavie Valsa

First Printed in United Kingdom 2019

Published by Conscious Dreams Publishing
www.consciousdreamspublishing.com

Edited by Lee Dickinson

Typeset by Oksana Kosovan

Photo Credit Caio Sanfelice
Instagram: @sanfelicecaio

ISBN: 978-1-912551-70-5

Dedication

I would like to dedicate this book to my parents. They have been so loving and supportive. The love I carry is because of them. I am made of love and now I want to share it with the world.

This book is for everyone who feels lost but wants to be found, feels ashamed but wants to be proud, is sad but wants to be happy, is confused but wants to see and feel things clearly.
This book is for everyone who is looking for a happy life, for the better self, anyone willing to take the happy roller coaster, enjoy the journey and share happiness with others. May this book help you to love yourself every single day, because I love you so much already.

Contents

What does Happiness Mean to Me?

Happiness is
when I'm not worried
about anything and I don't
feel any pain.
I'm just fully present
and smiling.
I'm thankful for that moment
and appreciate everything
that life provides me.

Introduction

Ok, so I was twenty-one when I first started writing this book. I wrote my last word at 24. I started after a year of constant thinking about it. I had so many thoughts last year that I couldn't keep them in my head any more; they needed to get out. Firstly, it started with quotes and ideas. I just wrote them down, but then it got to the point I had too many, so I decided to write a book. I'm writing this before the actual book and I have so much ahead, but I believe! These are the first words of my book. I really feel I have an important mission; a mission to spread the word across the planet, to inspire people, share happiness everywhere.

I want to help those who are in their teens or twenties, because that is the time when we start exploring ourselves. We have our whole life ahead of us, so it's a great opportunity to get ready for the big roller coaster. And, maybe because I'm that age and I'm talking from my experience, you'll believe my opinions more than if you heard it from your parents or grandparents, who do have more experience, but you don't really take them seriously because you think you still have some time to figure it all out on our own.

Before you start reading, I want to tell you that all my theories are based on my life experiences; everything that's been around me, all the quotes I've seen online, in the books, magazines and articles followed by my beliefs, thoughts and opinions. Maybe this book will be nothing new for you, maybe you've already seen or heard most of my words before. The aim of this book is to put all of my thoughts together into a simple summary. Sometimes books were really hard for me to understand; so many long phrases, endless chapters and, at the end, I was confused and didn't know what those previous twenty pages were all about. I want to make this book easy for you, so you can clearly understand and learn that the key to a happy life is not hard at all if you follow my simple advice.

The great thing about this book is that you can skip the chapters. The last chapter is as important, or interesting, as the first one. You don't need to read chronologically; if you see any chapter that catches your eye, just read it. I want to make the reading process as simple as possible for you, especially if you are not a big reader. I am not a big reader myself. All of my chapters are very short, sometimes just on one page, so enjoy it!

I am writing this book in my second language – English. I chose English because, despite the beauty of my mother tongue, the Czech language, English has a kind of ease and lightness that helps me to express my feelings. I am originally from Czechia, and although my English is 'advanced' now I'm twenty-one, I want to challenge myself and not wait until my English is perfect (I will talk about the word 'perfect' in-depth later) to write a book. So this is my language and grammar level right now, and I know when I look back in a few years I will see some mistakes, but I will know I tried my best with what I knew. This is my own masterpiece, and I believe in it.

Another fact is that because I don't have a computer or laptop; I'm writing everything on my mobile phone. It would be a bad excuse if I said: 'I couldn't write the book because my pen writing is too slow and my phone too small'. If you have been receiving any signs (like I was hearing my inner voice about doing this) that you should start doing something to show your true potential, do it! **Please** do it. It is true that it's hard to start, to finally sit down and decide what it is you want to do. The moment of decision, that's the most important one. The decision that the belief in your head is much stronger than any uncertainty, any doubtful people, any negative thoughts. Look at me, I haven't studied journalism, philosophy or psychology; I'm just following the voice in my head telling me to write, inspire, motivate, make people happier.

If you believe and you can imagine you will get there (in my case I believed I'd finish this book), you will, and you will find the most satisfying feeling ever.

About the book

I've always known I've got something (well, we all do, as you'll find later). I've always loved my life and was happy to be alive. I always felt lucky and my friends would call me very mature for my age or a magnet for success. I've never questioned why or whether I deserved that, or who I inherited that feeling of life force from. I'm only twenty-one, but I've been slowly uncovering the answers for a happy life.

The reason I'm writing this book, except those beliefs and missions, is a desire to help people around my age, because I will point at situations and possible opportunities that happen around the teenage years and our twenties. I want you to find the best version of yourself in you. I want you to feel special, loved, amazing and gifted. This book is called *Twenties and Happy* because twenty was the age when I realised it is possible to be happy at a young age and you don't have to wait until a certain age or a phase in your life when you think you'll achieve happiness.

If you're not in your twenties but you're still willing to learn how to live a happy life, please feel free to continue, don't think it's too late. This book has so much advice that can be practised at any age, and you never know how many beautiful years you might have ahead. So, no matter how old you are, how spiritual you are, how happy you are, you can start living a happy life right now.

CHAPTER ONE

HAPPINESS NOW

No matter if you are fifteen or fifty-one, you can be happy now. The circumstances and experiences might be different, you might be wiser when you get older, but the happy core inside you stays the same.

I always thought I'd be happy when I reached a certain point of my life. I imagined myself being fifty, having my business and drinking whiskey in my fancy gown while watching the snow falling from my luxurious apartment in New York at night. I thought this would be the peak of my happiness. It's been around six years since I thought that and 'planned' my happy future.

I've realised happiness doesn't come with age. It's an instant experience you can create no matter how old you are. I really think there is something beautiful about young happy people who have their own opinion about life and perceptions. I love seeing people the same age as me or younger being happy with their lives and smiling wherever they go.

From my own experience, I know my smile somehow attracts people around me, and they almost seem to be surprised because they're meeting someone who's been on this planet for only two decades yet is happy already with what they have.

I've been watching people a lot, and I realised one thing. There are more older people who smile than younger people. And one of the most common reasons for that is that my young friends think happiness will come to them when they get older, settle down, have lots of money to spend; you know, THINGS. I'd like to show them every experience hides a piece of happiness within, whether you're young or old.

CHAPTER TWO

I FOUND MY PURPOSE
ON THIS PLANET

Finding my purpose gave me a big reason to be happy and to live the life that gives me joy. I've learnt I need to live the life I want every day. I can't be happy only when I achieve my goal or celebrate my success; I want to be happy all the time between those 'very happy moments'. The secret is to fulfil my purpose, to live my truth, to celebrate every day of my life because I have the reason. When we look back at our lives, we would like to see the whole picture, right? By the picture, I mean every single day of our lives that makes a story. What would you like your story to be called? What do you live for? What do you believe in? What is the deep passion in your bones?

We need to find our purpose and live it as much as we can. Our purpose is the fuel that keeps us moving, gives us energy even when we are exhausted or we think we can't go further. We just need to find out what it is.

Shortly after my twentieth birthday, I realised my life purpose was to inspire people, to help people and to share happiness, joy and positivity around me. I realised I had a gift to make the world a better, happier place. I have a gift to heal it. Also, I knew it wouldn't happen in one week, and I knew it wouldn't happen globally overnight. It needed to start somewhere, though, so I began to write inspirational quotes, to connect with people, really listen to how they felt, what made them happy and what their dreams were. I started to smile at strangers more often. Wherever I went, I was the happiest person in the room; I spread my happy mood everywhere I went and felt the place became much happier. I just need to know everything is all right and everyone feels good.

I know it's my choice to take responsibility for the environment I'm in, to make sure I feel great and people around me do as well. By supporting people, making them happy, believing in them, being kind to everyone around me and gentle to the planet, I leave traces of my magical dust behind me (you have it too). I plant a little seed of happiness in everyone I meet, knowing I've left an impact on them, that I inspired them and they're going to wake up tomorrow spreading the seed to their family, friends or co-workers, further and further. Because we are all connected, we can create a beautiful, happy, peaceful and kind world to live in.

Once we know our purpose, we need to chase it and pay attention to it.

Let's say your purpose is peace for the rest of your life. Firstly, you'd avoid any stressful situations, people, violence, a hectic lifestyle. Secondly, you'd start chasing peace in you and around you, start meditating, focusing on your breath, being mindful. You'd move to the countryside, somewhere nice and quiet where your peace wouldn't be disturbed. If your life purpose is to travel, it'd start with looking at a map the whole time, taking adventurous trips around your hometown and later spending all your money on holidays and exploring the world.

To sum it up, we need to listen to our instinct, to observe what we really love, to find our purpose and then spend some time with it and later enjoy the sweetness of our reward, accomplishment and pure happiness.

CHAPTER THREE

DECISIONS

When we are young and full of dreams, we need to decide what to do and where to go. We have lots of decisions ahead and, sometimes, it can be hard to decide what steps to take.

I have advice for the times when you don't know what to do. If you are deciding which way to go, ask yourself how you will look at this situation and this moment in one week or a few years. This will help you to understand the perspective of time, and it will feel more relaxed in the future than right now because you are under pressure and not sure what to do. So, when you look back in few years, what can you see? How do you feel? What emotions are going through your head? Are you happy with your decision or do you have regrets because you would've changed some things?

I try to listen to my instincts. My instincts tell me what to do, and sometimes I even feel like I'm not the one who makes decisions; it almost feels like there are many little strings connecting me to The Source, like there is someone manipulating me and telling me what to do, just like a puppet. In these cases, I have a feeling of security and absolute certainty the direction I'm going in is right.

CHAPTER FOUR

MINDSET

Happiness is not given – happiness is chosen

Well, the attitude of happiness is. When you wake up in the morning, don't hope for a happy day, choose a happy day! With a happy mindset, you can go through the whole day smoothly with a smile. Every day, we are responsible for our next twenty-four hours, We can wake up and say to ourselves: 'I'm gonna have a great day!' Or we can say: 'Omg, it's gonna be a horrible day, a stressful day, an awful day, a hectic day, a day full of annoying people etc.'

In my chapter 'Affirmations', I talk about creating a life we want. With affirmations, we can create the life/day we desire. One of my most common affirmations for a perfect day sounds something like this: 'I go through my day with a smile, ease, light heart and I'm grateful for anything I receive today. I accept all circumstances that happen to me today because I know everything is happening for my biggest good.

I'm kind to everyone and everyone is kind to me. I flow through my day with harmony and passion for things I love. I appreciate every moment I get to experience.'

When negativity tries to bring you down right after you wake up, firstly ask yourself:

- What am I worried about today?
- What am I nervous about today?
- Who or what am I mad at today?
- What am I negative about in general?

Once you know the answers, find a positive contrast to it. For example, if you are concerned about your work meetings and you don't feel confident in front of others, or you feel insecure to work with other people, your morning affirmation could sound something like this: 'I am a confident person. I act professionally in front of other people and I'm respected and appreciated. I handle every situation and I communicate with people smoothly.'

The more often you realise you're finding yourself wrapped in negative thoughts, the more often you step back and start thinking about the positive option, the more often you start using a positive attitude, the happier your life will be. You'll start believing in yourself more and worrying less. You'll be more confident, radiant and less doubtful.

Everything is OK

Knowing everything we are going through is right for us is a freeing feeling that makes us feel calm because we are sure we walk the right path (our path). We are responsible for choices we make and we always try to make the best decisions in the moment based on how we feel and what we believe in. Looking back and regretting our decisions won't only make no difference to your past, but it will also waste your time in the present.

In some life situations, when we can't make choices, we need to believe our life source (our Creator or anything you believe created us) is pulling us in the right direction and all the obstacles are actually blessings, lessons or skills that we will need later, so we can reach our potential and our supreme destiny. It's like floating in the sea; if we get scared, we hold tension in our body and drown, but if we let it go and trust, we start to float on the water without any help. All we need to do is to give up any worries, tension, stress or inner fights and just surrender to the creator that's planned our amazing life.

CHAPTER FIVE

IT IS OUR HUMAN RIGHT
TO FEEL GOOD

I was worrying about my future, about my money, about the people I was going to meet, even about my look and how I appeared to others. I was living in tension for a long time: worrying, planning, hesitating, still living under pressure.

Suddenly, something amazing happened. I went for a walk. I can't remember whether it was the sunrise or sunset. I was walking down the street, thinking about my life and suddenly it all hit me: I got lost in the power of the nature. I could feel the breeze in my hair, I saw the bright shades of green, I could smell the salty ocean air. I felt free and deeply connected to nature. In that moment, I realised it is OK to feel good. I realised I'm not my thoughts, I'm not living in tomorrow; that moment I was in the NOW and I promised myself I wouldn't feel guilty for feeling good any more. I'll start feeling good at any time, and try to make a habit of feeling good as often as I can. I know feeling good about ourselves and our lives is our human right; it is a necessity leading to a happy life. Let's celebrate our life cheerfully: 'Wake up, feel good, go to sleep, repeat!'

We are not here to suffer, feel guilty or be hurt by others. We are here to dance, enjoy, celebrate every day and see joy wherever we go.

CHAPTER SIX

AFFIRMATIONS

It was Louise L Hay who was responsible for the beginning of my wellbeing/positive life journey. I remember when I was seventeen, my mum gave me Louise's little book with 365 positive affirmations, one for every day, and I read them and loved them so much. I would call this period a breaking point in my life, because the person I am today was made somewhere around seventeen, when my spiritual (r)evolution started.

I believe in the power of affirmations so much. In the beginning, an affirmation can seem ridiculous or funny or impossible but, with time, you will change your mind because you'll start seeing a significant difference in your life, especially in the conversation between you and your mind. Now it's been more than four years since I started practising affirmations and using them in my everyday life. So many times I have been happy, calm or confident just because of them. Affirmations will stop you being anxious about your future because they are practised in the present sense, so instead of 'I'll be successful', I'm saying 'I am successful' (This has been my most used affirmation since I was seventeen, by the way).

Affirmations are a skill, like any other. They take time and practice. In the beginning, I was just reading them, and didn't believe in them because it seemed so unnatural to say, 'Wherever I go there is beauty and harmony'. But I knew I had to give it a chance. A little later, I started to memorise some of my favourite affirmations, the part of my life I wanted to focus on (it was mostly success, relationships with other people and abundance) and, finally, I started putting affirmations into my life based on what I needed to achieve or where I wanted to get. But, mostly, I started believing in them.

Nowadays, I accept my favourite affirmation, 'I am successful'. I believe in it and don't even think about it, therefore I see success in everything I touch or everywhere I go. This feeling gives me happiness, a feeling of accomplishment and fulfilment in my life; I'm not feeling stressed that I'm not where I want to be or that I'll be successful only when I achieve this or that when I'm forty years old. I think we shouldn't wait any longer to feel we are enough. We are on top of the world right now, doing our best, living our lives right now, so affirmations in the present sense really help us to keep living the perfect life we've always dreamt about. Any affirmation will help you to be happy where you are and live the life you want to live. So, whatever you want to improve or change and you believe you can, write it down and get it into your subconscious mind.

Shortly after I moved to London, I wrote this in my phone:

'I have a part-time job I love and enjoy and I'm being paid at least £10 an hour.

I have a big beautiful room for myself for maximum £150 a week very close to public transport, easy to commute with clean housemates and beautiful interior.

I am a popular London performer.

I perform in London twice a week.

I make £500 a week.

I am a busy and popular make-up artist in London.

I am loved.'

Most of the affirmations came true within two months of writing them down.

Of course, later, I had more to achieve, higher standards and ambitions, which is OK. We just need to make affirmations for the near future and work with what we have. For example, your affirmation can't be, 'I am excellent at playing hockey' if you don't train enough. It obviously takes some work to go towards your goal but, once you start working on it, the affirmation comes along and intensifies your ability or talent or anything you want to do or achieve.

I believe in something so much that I repeat it and think about it until I can see it or feel I have it. Also, I really believe the universe works with me, not against me, tries to help me with every affirmation and, if there is an affirmation I'm using to get something I really want but the universe thinks I don't need it, I usually get something even better or something I had no idea about before.

CHAPTER SEVEN

KNOW YOU SHINE AND
YOU ARE BEAUTIFUL

P lease remember this: You are beautiful and you matter! You are so beautiful, you are important and you shine. Why? Because you were born. The fact you are on this world is enough to know how irreplaceable you are. I really wish everyone found their beauty and light.

Imagine all the darkness around you and you are the lighthouse, shining bright everywhere around you, and there are ships (other people) who look for YOUR light. It's your unique light they wouldn't find at any other lighthouse; they need YOUR special kind of light.

Even if you think no one knows about you, you still need to know how important you are in this world. We are all influencers, by our acts of kindness (or hate), our words, our speech and behaviour. We leave a mark behind us, we inspire others, showing them how to be the best version of themselves (or how to not be). We make a significant difference in each person's life every day. Imagine you meet ten people a day and make an impact on them. They can meet another ten people that day and, because they are moved by your acts of kindness or your unique look or the way you were expressing yourself, they will remember and spread it further and further. Without you being there or even having an idea, something you did based on your best knowledge and deepest truth could be shared by tens of other people. You are the brightest star in many eyes, even if they don't tell you.

We might be brought down through the day, feel insecure, or people can tell us we are not pretty enough or smart enough or our ideas are bad. This shouldn't matter, because we know what message we have for the world, and if others don't like it, they might not be ready for it or they are not the right people to work with. I always remember if ten people say NO to me it's because there is the eleventh person who's gonna say YES, and we might build a beautiful relationship, partnership, friendship. We might start a project together, introduce other interesting and inspiring people to each other. The people might turn our lives upside down, inside out, and we'll start being grateful for those ten people who said no because, without them, we wouldn't be living our best life right now.

It is so important to believe in us, our importance, our dreams, the mission we know we have, and not to get distracted by the opinions of others. Our faith and belief can produce magic once we figure out why we are walking this planet, and what mark should remain here after us.

CHAPTER EIGHT

PURPOSE

Have you ever asked yourself: 'What am I doing here? Why am I on this planet? What should I leave behind?' You are here to find out what your purpose is. Deep inside of you is the answer. It's been within you since you were born. You might not know it yet. You still might be on your journey finding your purpose, finding what's really important to you, what you are truly convinced about. You know you just should do something.

Don't worry. You don't need to know that today. It took me a few years before I realised I am here to help people, to make the world a better place, to make people a little bit happier, to make brighter any place I go. I finally realised I was born for people; to motivate them, to give them advice and answer their spiritual questions. Your purpose doesn't need to be an important mission to save the world.

(Although everyone is here to save the world, as we are irreplaceable parts of the galaxy. You might say some people damage our planet, kill people, steal or lie. The truth is, they are here to show us, to teach us how we can make the world a better, safer, more loving and more beautiful place. There is no creature that shouldn't have been born. They are all here to accomplish their purpose. And if it's positive or negative to you, that doesn't matter.) You can peacefully live all your life lonely, without anyone. The purpose doesn't have to be for people, or for the world. Purpose was given to you to teach why you, the body made of billions of cells, were created to start, make or finish something very important. You are the whole that connects all the beings and galaxies together.

My purpose is to make the world a happier place. I was born to shine and make all life's creatures happy. I have explored my inner power, my strength and qualities. I love being happy, smiling even without a reason, just to gently assure everyone that it is all good right now; there are no worries, no stress, all we can do is to smile at any time! I don't need to put any effort into my happy personality any more; it becomes more and more automatic, so it's an absolutely natural thing to me.

CHAPTER NINE

SMILE

S preading good vibes and making everybody feel good and comfortable is one of the best qualities you can have. People around you will feel better and they'll smile more. And guess what!? Smiling is catchy! So the more people you make smile, the more smiles they're going to spread around them, therefore you'll make the world a better, happier place. Really, don't forget you are responsible for the happy world around you.

I smile as long as I can and I think that's the best advice for a happy life. You are the one who decides whether you want to smile or not, you are the one who is responsible for your happiness and, therefore, your happy life. Did you know that just by smiling at yourself in the morning, you trigger happiness hormones in your body and you become instantly happier and your chance to have a happy day is increased? If you feel down, just smile and see what happens.

Most of the time I walk down the street and smile at every passing stranger. When I was a kid, I read somewhere: 'Be the one who smiles first.' Since then it's been stuck in my head, I try to share my inner happiness with everyone and to spread it at as many places as I can. I believe once you find your inner joy and the inner power that has been within you, you will start realising how easy it is to pass it to others. Whether I smile at people on the streets or waiters at cafes or passengers on the bus, I always get a warm, rewarding feeling, and I'll tell you why. Firstly, most of the people smile back at you, which is very beautiful, and somehow you feel such a nice connection with the whole world because, suddenly, it makes you feel that you are the one who is contributing to the whole world's happiness. Secondly, even when people don't smile at you, you get that beautiful feeling anyway because, by deciding you are going to smile, you automatically make yourself feel strong because you had the courage and made the effort to do so.

The quote: 'Be the reason someone smiles today[1]' doesn't involve only cases where you can see instant feedback of someone smiling at you in the street. Even when you don't see people smiling back at you, don't worry, they see that. They might not smile at you straight away, but they surely will be carrying the memory of your smile for the rest of the day, because you've brightened their day.

---

1   unknown author

Here are a few reasons people don't smile at you straight away:

- they smile on the inside but you can't see that
- they passed by too fast to have time to smile
- they might be lazy about moving their facial muscles
- they simply don't feel like smiling

Sometimes I even cry when an old lady smiles back at me; the gesture of kindness and her life story says it all. A smile is the best outfit you can ever wear, so why not wear it every day?

CHAPTER TEN

DREAMS

I would define the word 'dream' as something like: an exciting hope that something wonderful will happen to us; a belief that our experience will be even more contented. When a dream comes true, we have a warm feeling of satisfaction that creates happiness.

A dream is a sweet memory of future. We love to hope and think there are even better moments and better times and something more beautiful that feels even better than we feel right now. It's the excitement that good times are coming; even though we should appreciate where we are right now, we definitely should hope something bright and beautiful is about to come.

We all have dreams. We all want to have a beautiful future, achieve goals, have successful careers, ideal partners. Sometimes dreams come true in a few days, sometimes in years. Sometimes we have to try so hard. Sometimes we don't need to do anything, just let it go, have the right intentions and life will reward us.

CHAPTER ELEVEN

CONTROL OF YOUR MIND

This is the important one. Every thought you have is actually an illusion of your current reality, and it's based on your knowledge, mood, beliefs, experiences... the ones you've had until now.

For instance, you were born into a family where rich people were bad and didn't treat others right, had unnecessarily big properties and useless, fast cars. You thought that it's not good to be rich, so you've been living with this thought for ten, twenty years, and you know what you would do with the money. You have good intentions, but because your family told you all those negative things, you stop chasing your ambitions and stay on their opinion level.

But you have the choice to change your decision – guess where?! Your thoughts. You've certainly heard you can achieve whatever you want. And you really can. So you became rich, wrecked all the mindset formulas and started to believe in whatever you can, do whatever you want and live a truly free and happy life.

Or, if you are a minority and you are trying to get into some industry or a field where no minorities like you made it before, you might feel frustrated and hear the voices in your head that tell you reasons you shouldn't get there. But, again, you are the one who can change that; you create your reality, and your way of thinking will or won't get you where you desire to go. For example, if you are a transgender person like me, and no trans person has ever hosted the main news on TV, you can do it. If you believe it, you can achieve it.

Whatever I focus on and set my mind to, I can achieve it. When I'm writing this book, I know I'll finish it without doubts; I strongly believe there is no way other than getting my book published. I don't worry about the circumstances. I have the reason, the meaning, the passion for it, so I know there is no way but to make it happen.

CHAPTER TWELVE

INSTINCTS

There is not a worse feeling than doing something we feel that isn't right, spending our time with people we feel are wasting our time, places we feel we don't belong, work we don't like. If you feel like there is something more important or useful to do, always follow the voice of your heartbeat and do the things that are important to you. When you have an instinct that is telling you to do this or that, you need to follow that to give your life a smooth flow, because if you hide or ignore your instinct, you often end up hurting yourself because your heart hasn't met the fulfilment it has been seeking.

For example, if your instinct is telling you to not hang out with that person but you keep hanging out with them, you end up scarred at the end because, most probably, the person is not good for you, or has bad intentions or can be fake and talk behind your back.

In my case, my body sometimes tells me not to drink coffee, because I feel sick after and my stomach doesn't want any food, but my brain is telling me: 'Try the coffee; it's from this famous roasting company and this is the only time you can try it.' It does this even though I don't feel like drinking coffee, so it's the same thing with instincts and your inner voice and connection to your body.

Remember, an instinct equals nothing but pure truth. If your instinct persists in putting you in a certain direction that all people around you don't want you to go, just leave (I'm not saying don't listen to them, because there people who matter who care and who love you, but there is a difference between listening to their ideas on how you should live and your idea, your heart, your dreams and your instinct!). Say no to their plans; it is your life, right?

Imagine you leave your town tomorrow. Are the opinions of all the people you've left behind important now? You are responsible for your decisions and your happiness, so follow your instincts, go where your soul desires, take the first step if you think it's the right one. Make the decision that will benefit you and people around you and you'll be happy tomorrow, no matter what, because you'll be lighter. Lighter of the feeling to please others.

CHAPTER THIRTEEN

HEAR YOUR CALLING

Your calling (you can also call it your inner voice) was there within you since you were born. When you are little, you know you want to become someone; a professional, usually. But how do you know it? Who told you that? Where did you hear about it to make you want to do it so much? It is a desire, and a desire comes from your heart. You can't build or practise desire, you can only follow it. And when you know you really want something, your desire takes over and leads you towards your dream.

Your calling is the same; it is within you and you can't obtain it from any other source but you. It's when you know you really should start a new business with shoes; when you know you should move to America; when you know you should start playing drums. This is when you listen to your inner voice that tells you what next. While I'm writing this, I realised you can also call it your instinct. It's the next step you want to take, the decision you want to make. It is all based on your instinct. When you listen to your instinct, you get somewhere you need to be. It is the calling that draws you toward it.

You won't always understand why you are going through an uncomfortable or painful experience when you were listening to your instincts and following your calling. It will be unclear and you might be confused, but then something beautiful will happen and all the question marks will become clear and you will be in the next chapter, on another path towards your calling.

I'll share one of my stories with you. When I lived in Sydney, my instinct was telling me to move to LA. I felt Sydney was too small for me; it felt like I had done it all, explored it all and it felt like the right time to move on. I was receiving so many signs about the US, about California, about Los Angeles; everything around me indicated that my next stop must be LA. So I left Sydney, because I knew I needed to leave. I was sure about LA, so sure.

At the border control in LA, the police stopped me and took me to the side. My visa was showing I was going to stay there for exactly 90 days which is allowed on a tourist visa. However when they asked me how much money I had, I answered $1000 which was true but obviously not enough to travel around America for three months. Once they went through my phone, because I was suspicious, they found conversations between my dad and I where I'd explained that I was planning to stay forever. I spent two days in jail, during the day in the airport, during the night in Beverly

Hills, so the only piece of an American land I saw was sunrise through the bars or the police car. They wanted to send me back to Sydney, but I told them I didn't want to go to there, and I didn't have any extra money, so they deported me to Czechia because my passport was Czech. This was the last place I wanted to end up. I was depressed for three months, locked in my room, didn't want to see my friends and family and was so confused because I really believed in my dream and I just knew LA was my future. I had no idea what to do with my life, particularly where to live. London was the only option.

Now, when I look back, I see why this all happened. The reason I'm living my dream life in London right now is because I was listening to my inner voice and I was brave enough to follow it. I did end up in jail and confused in Czechia for three months, but without that I would still be stuck in Sydney (as much as I love Sydney and Australia is my home, career-wise it wasn't for me at that time). When I look back, all the struggle and pain were a part of my inner calling, my journey.

Our calling is changing with the years depending on our needs, situations and spiritual development. But it is always there.

My calling right now is to write a book. I have had too much on my mind the last two years, so I decided to write it out; my opinions, ideas, outlooks. I understand my calling as a mission. It's a mission to spread the word, to make the world a happier place. That's what I reply when someone asks me: 'Hey, what do you do?' I answer: 'I make the world a happier place.' It is hard to ignore your calling; it is hard to cover your ears or eyes and pretend you can't hear or see it. Your calling is deep within you. It is there.

Whenever I want to watch a movie, my calling just doesn't want to. I literally can hear: 'Pavie, stop this, write your book, share your word, people need you.' It is impossible to ignore your calling even when it's not pleasant or comfortable or, in my case, easy. I don't want to sit down and write a book because it's more fun. I know it is easier to watch the movie or scroll on my Insta, but I just need to get it done. It is stronger than me.

What is your calling? What do you think your mission is? What is it that needs to be done?

CHAPTER FOURTEEN

GRATITUDE

O h, my favourite one. And to me it's actually the easiest way to create that happy feeling immediately. When we realise how lucky and blessed we are, we won't be sad any more. So, how to be grateful and what actually is gratitude? The funny thing is that we can be grateful everywhere! Because there is always a reason to be grateful.

Senses:

The easiest and fastest way to start being grateful is through our senses. When we engage our senses, we start to feel everything more intensely. The most common reason to be grateful is breathing. When I'm breathing, I feel alive, and I say thank you to the Creator of my life and of every life on this planet. My breathing always reminds me how fragile I am and how precious life is because anything can happen and the next minute is not guaranteed, so I often stop, put my right palm on my heart, and then I am still and humble, grateful for my functioning body and for being alive.

We can do the same with our hearing, especially among nature. We can really connect with nature by listening to her and how she's talking to us; the sound of the leaves when it's breezy, birds singing, you name it. When I can hear that, I admire all the sounds I can experience that moment (my best friend, Chrisen, gave me a great tip on how to meditate: Close your eyes and all you need to do is count noises. Count anything you can hear and deeply focus on every sound. It makes you present in the moment by recognising and paying attention to all the sounds). At those moments, I feel I'm part of the living and constantly evolving environment.

My sight also gives me an immediate feeling of gratitude. Sometimes I just stop and I realise: 'Omg, I can see, my brain is absorbing all of this and I can see it all!' There is so much beauty around us every single moment. We can enjoy colours, shapes, sizes and admire it all. When I look around, I'm grateful, saying to myself: 'Oh, what a beautiful world I have around.' If I was blind I wouldn't be able to see the smiles people give me or the clouds that pass in the blue sky, I wouldn't see the bright green colour of trees in the spring. And that's a big reason to be grateful.

It's the same with all our other senses. Often I'm grateful for my sense of smell, as I'm very sensitive to all the smells, and they bring me back to a memory, make me feel happy, sad, emotional, nostalgic. The sense of smell is wonderful and a big reason to be grateful.

Appreciation:

The second thing that makes me feel immediately grateful, after my senses, is to realise where I am and what I'm going through right now. Whenever I want to complain about my financial situation or the environment I am in, I ask: 'Do I have a comfortable bed and a roof over my head? Can I eat today? Am I healthy and is my body functioning well? Am I, or my family and friends, safe without fear of being attacked by bombs?' Thankfully, most of the time, the answer to all these questions is 'Yes'. After these questions I forget the uncomfortable mattress at the hotel, the almond milk instead of soya milk in my flat white, the jacket I don't want to wear because it's last season. I simply start to be grateful where I am and be happy with what I have.

The end of the day:

Do you ever feel so happy at the end of the day because you simply had so much beauty around you? You feel lucky, you feel blessed, someone made you smile, you made someone else smile, you visited some beautiful new place, you exercised, did something for your body, learnt something new. Basically, you experienced a pure form of happiness and you feel so grateful that you're just smiling and feeling on top of the world. Lots of people actually keep a gratitude journal where they write three things they are grateful for that day. I think it's a brilliant idea on how to stay grateful every day.

CHAPTER FIFTEEN

SELF-CARE

Body nourishment:

I see my body as my best friend, as someone I'm nice, kind and respectful to. Let's keep a dialogue with our body, ask if it needs any help, if the food we eat makes us feel great.

I used to try so many diets to not just keep my body healthy, but also get into my dream shape. I wanted to look like an aesthetic model. I tried carb cycling, paleo diet, dairy free. I did get some results, but then I realised one thing; I was doing all the portion control, scheduled eating and no carbs before sleep just to look great on the outside. I forced myself to have eggs and a full plate of vegetables in the morning even though it made me feel sick. I didn't care about my best friend (my body) that didn't feel good, that wanted help. Therefore, I wasn't happy. I was hungry in the morning just because I stopped myself having a slice of bread, even though my body felt like that. It takes time to figure out what foodstuffs make you feel great, satisfied and happy. You can eat anything your body craves as long as it doesn't have a harmful impact on your health. Recently I've been realising that if I have everything in moderation, I'm happy.

Sometimes we feel miserable; tired, without any motivation, lazy and procrastinating. Well, one probable reason can be that we haven't put our body in motion for ages. Find ANYTHING that makes you move, if it makes you sweaty, even better. Find out whether you prefer training in the morning, jogging in the park or a treadmill, jumping the skipping rope, listening to the music or birds, doing yoga on your own or with a partner. After a physical activity, our body exudes hormones, endorphins that create a happy state of mind. It feels amazing! It's important to train your muscles and get flexibility. PS: Most of my book was written after a physical activity, and I also wrote positive quotes. I guess there is something about that, huh? Your body will be grateful when you get older. Be wise with anything you put into your body. Imagine your body is an engine; the more careful and loving you are, the stronger it works and the longer it endures. I remember an interview with a ninety-year-old lady where she shared her advice for longevity and vitality in her nineties: 'Use it or you'll lose it.'

Soul nourishment:

We need to take care not only of our physical body but also our spiritual one. We need to nourish our soul as much as our body. We should be gentle to ourselves and not put our beautiful soul under pressure. By surrounding ourselves with beautiful things, like books, music, pictures, nature, friends and family, positive quotes, things we love, travelling, meditation etc, we feed our soul and make it happier and happier. I nourish my soul by surrounding myself with things that I love and I'm passionate about. Sometimes I forget to eat; I forget my responsibilities just because my soul is in a happy place. The next chapter will show you how important it is to nourish your soul and keep yourself happy.

Favourite things:

If we want a happy life, we should do things that make us happy. We should ask ourselves: 'What do I love? What makes me feel good?'

In my case, I love talking about the universe on the beach while watching the stars, touching someone's ears, listening to summer house music while drinking fresh coconut juice by the ocean, doing yoga and big brunches on Sundays, reading books in a hammock, walking barefoot in the grass or sand, dancing, singing, painting, going out and feeling fabulous. I love men, making others happier, green hills in the country. Almost all of these things we can do for free; we need just ourselves.

If you haven't done any of your favourite things recently, do them right now. Yes, right now! Look around and find anything satisfying. It will make you smile, and you will feel amazing. It can be just your favourite meal, jumping on your bed, scratching your foot, smelling fresh towels. Eventually, try to do something passionate every day, maybe every hour. It takes you a just few seconds and makes the next moments of your day much more enjoyable, and you'll become happier.

People often ask me: 'What do you do for living and what are your hobbies?' I have plenty of hobbies, and I'm so lucky to say that my work is a hobby too. It's doing make-up, performing, entertaining, writing, travelling, inspiring people. Basically doing what I enjoy, making people happier and being paid for that. Isn't it a great combination? What is it you love so much you need to do or you think about it every day? What are you really good at? What could you learn even more so you can become the best in your field? If you really see a meaning in what you do and you become very good at it, people will pay you for it, and you'll find the perfect balance between work and your hobbies. Actually, you'll create balance, and everything will be in harmony because the energy you put out there (your time, work, effort, patience) you'll get back (money, new friends, creating a circle of people who love the same thing, travelling, help from others, invitations to events you are interested in, but mostly the satisfying feeling).

CHAPTER SIXTEEN

SELF-LOVE

We all are different. Every single one. We might look different, come from a different country, culture, religion. We might have different gifts, different circumstances in our lives, we might speak a different language, but the truth is we all speak the same language; the language of love and understanding.

We should be proud of ourselves, be proud of who we are, to whom we were born and remember who we were when we woke up this morning. We should love ourselves. Just as we are not wishing to be, look or behave like someone else, neither should we compare our skills, body, achievements with anyone. In fact, comparing is the biggest thief of our self-love and our happiness. If we compare, we wish to be this and that and we start to think we are not beautiful enough, chatty enough, friendly enough, or our skills at work are not enough.

We see animals in nature and they are all different. We love the way they look, we admire them, see every part of their bodies as beautiful. We love the oldest elephant as much as the calf. We love the ginger, brown and black monkey the same, right? They don't wish to be like the other animals, they just simply exist; they eat, they hang out and they are happy.

Then we see people in the streets. We start to judge them and compare them with the ideal (face, body shape, ideal couples, ideal measurements, social norms) of something that doesn't even exist, something that was just made up by humans. We stop seeing the beauty of/in every human being, their gifts, colours, shapes, features, the unique parts of everyone. We tend to put others in boxes and put labels on them (black, white, Asian, gay, trans, poor, rich, beautiful, ugly).

We do the same thing to ourselves. You may think you're not good enough for someone or something, not talented enough, not clever enough, not tall enough, not beautiful enough. It's all the chaos around you that has confused you, my love. You are just perfect as you are, you don't need to change a thing. Nothing!

You stand here with me, with everyone else, and I will give you all I have to make you love yourself. Just close your eyes, if you can, put your palms on your heart, feel the beat, feel the circulating blood, the moving lungs; everything has been moving and working so preciously. Can you feel the love your body's giving you? Your body loves you, your soul loves you and you, a soul, love your body. You are happy to be alive, you are amazed how everything is working and you start to understand your uniqueness. You start to see that you're not here to be a copy of someone famous or someone who is the 'ideal'; that doesn't even exist. You know you are here in your own beauty, your truth, your divine energy and your light that is so important here for everyone. Remember, if you accept your body, your behaviour, your culture, your characteristic features that everyone knows you for, you will start to feel so important and irreplaceable, so unique, and you will know that you're the one and only! Love yourself and show everyone how beautiful self-love is and how much happiness it brings into your life. Self-love is catchy; people will see your confidence and brightness and they'll want it too, and you can tell them how easy it is.

CHAPTER SEVENTEEN

YOU ARE PERFECT

At the start of my book, I was talking about my English. I said 'I'm writing this book even though my English is not perfect yet.' By perfect, I mean I'm not a native English speaker, and I'll never be, but I improve and learn. Although I enjoy my journey of learning and I love my English as it is right now, I strongly believe my English actually is perfect right now, as it is – it is perfection, a perfection of my perfect evolution.

Perfect is the word that most people don't like because they think they're not perfect and they can't achieve it. I believe we are all perfect the way we are. We are already perfect for being who we are. The perfection we try to aim for and think is hard to achieve, that perfection is fake. It literally doesn't exist. Because perfection, whether it's the 'perfect' skin on the cover of the magazine (usually perfection is associated with beauty and looks, the impossible beauty society and the media wash our brains with) or the 'perfect' garden or the 'perfect' yoga pose or 'perfect' holidays, is nothing else but comparing our lives with others. Often it's trying to achieve the unachievable because all the beauty is photoshopped and all the pictures are an illusion. Your skin is perfect the way it is, your garden is beautiful, your yoga pose is good enough right now, your holidays are memorable.

The thing is, it's always good to aim higher and push ourselves towards our goals, be the better versions of ourselves than we were yesterday. Growth is necessary for our development in any field, but we should never compare our personal growth to others. We shouldn't strive for the perfection of others, but our own perfection. Our perfect life, perfect development, perfect environment, just how it is.

I no longer strive for perfection, because I know everything I'll do will be perfect the way it will be. I can always go higher than I was yesterday, I can always be the perfect version of me. I can get inspired by others, but if I'm trying to get exactly the same that others have, I usually don't succeed because I don't have the same qualities, opportunities and possibilities as them. But if I focus on that version of MY perfect life and my perfect goals, whatever the outcome might be, I'm happy with that because I was working on my own masterpiece, mastering my own kind of perfect.

CHAPTER EIGHTEEN

THE MAGIC OF THE MOMENT

Right now, I'm looking out of my window in my house on Oxford Street in Sydney. It's a warm autumn night, shortly before midnight. The cars are passing by and there is no one on the street; everyone is sleeping. It's a full moon tonight and I can't fall asleep. I'm inhaling the clean (post-traffic) air into my lungs so preciously, deeply and enjoying this moment of my lungs expanding, and I'm happy for the cells being fed by the oxygen I'm giving them with all my love.

I will always remember this night. Not just because I'm writing about that, but also because I feel this is the moment when I AM. I have so many memories from my childhood when I was falling asleep in my bed or sitting by the road, and I remember the moment I stopped noticing things and said to myself: 'This is the moment. This is a special time that one day you'll remember.' And I still do. Tonight is one of those special times.

Whenever I find myself under pressure or in a stressful situation I stop and:

1. Switch off
2. Take a deep breath
3. Relax my neck and shoulders and fix my posture
4. Realise where I am and look around me
5. Think of three things I'm grateful for
6. Smile for myself and remember I'm loved
7. Know my life is short and precious and every problem I might go through actually doesn't matter

It is a long journey. In fact, it's our whole-life obligation, to appreciate the present moment and be all there. Just be, realise where we are and enjoy everything we have around us. The present moment is irreplaceable; it is so precious because the future is not guaranteed and we would be silly to worry about it. Once we get to live this life, it is up to us how we manage it and how many precious moments we experience. We are directors of our own movies and are responsible for its course.

I've found out the true magic of the moment is hidden in things that make us happy and give us pleasure, so we feel everything more intensely and really are in the moment. For me, it's a walk in nature, feeling the sun on my face, having an orgasm, laughing with my best friend, hugging my family members, smiling at strangers, having a stretch, putting the first mouthful of my favourite food in my mouth, shavasana at the end of a yoga class, running through empty streets at night, seeing people smiling after giving them a gift or helping them. Precious moments like these make me happy and make my life beautiful.

When are you feeling alive? How does YOUR moment feel? What makes you be present and at peace with yourself? These questions are really worth asking as they help you discover yourself, who you are and your purpose on this planet.

CHAPTER NINETEEN

NO LIMITATIONS

I t took me a while before I realised there are no limits in my life.

There.
Are.
No.
Limits.

Everything you've learnt to this point of your life, you've learnt from someone, right? All the opinions of your friends and family, news on TV, cultural norms, how the universe works, traditions, moral standards. This has all been piling up in your head since you were born. You might agree with everything, you might not. However, those thoughts have a big impact on your life, on your personality, how you act around people, go out, express your true self.

How many times do you hear a family member's opinion in your head before you make an actual decision? In my case, I always hear my mum's voice saying: 'Isn't it too much?' when I'm trying on some sexy new clothes or lots of colourful combinations. Or, 'No, It's awkward,' when I'm about to ask someone for help. My mum never meant it in the wrong way, but because I heard it so many times as a kid, her opinions and words got stuck in my head and I still hear it now as an adult. Sometimes these thoughts used to limit me before I made my decision. It wasn't just my family, it was my friends, usually very conservative friends, and, because I'm naturally very confident and controversial and just out there, I found it an issue to truly express who I was without hearing their voice.

How many times have you remembered your friend's opinion (in the worst case, the media's, or someone that you don't look up to, someone you don't even know, someone who hasn't even met you) before dressing up for a party? And how many times have you listened to this voice and made a decision against your own will? There is nothing worse than living a limited life, sadly, limited not only by others, but often by our own thoughts.

So, remember; whatever you've learnt or heard or was taught to you, it is all up to you whether you accept it and believe it or if you don't and carry on in life with your own beliefs, your own opinions, your own theories.

Remember the people who tried to fly or make the first planes. They were often called crazy because, until that point, no one was flying, therefore everyone thought it was impossible. They were all limited because that's what they learnt and knew, but those who really believed in their dreams and believed it was possible to fly didn't think about their limits – they created their own reality.

Life really is limitless. What is it you believe you can do and you really want to start doing, but the limits of others keep you down? Come on, go out there and share your truth, your dreams and your passion. Don't limit yourself; trust yourself!

CHAPTER TWENTY

THE HAPPINESS OF GIVING

I know I am made of love to others. I love giving so much. When I was a child, and I'm pretty sure I'm not the only one, I was excited before every Christmas and my birthday because I knew I was going to get a toy or something I really wanted. Later, when I was a teenager, I started to give, because I was able to make a gift or sometimes even buy a gift. In the last few years (maybe it's my independence, because I make my own money and I can buy anything I want for myself), I don't look forward to my birthday or Christmas or any anniversaries because I'm expecting a gift from someone. I have changed my priorities, and I appreciate good company and seeing my family and friends much more than receiving a gift from them. But, mostly, I love to give presents to them. I love it when they open my gift and are truly happy and pleasantly surprised and their eyes are sparkling because they are so thankful and joyful.

The most beautiful way to give a gift is unexpectedly. Sometimes I bring chips or nuts to my co-workers, or I tell a funny joke to my best friend or buy someone flowers. Just because, without a reason. I love to see my favourite people happy whenever I can, not only for big celebrations, because every day is a reason to celebrate our friendship.

Of course, by giving, I don't mean only giving presents and material gifts. To me, giving is anything that involves our energy going towards someone else's energy. Giving is a beautiful thing, but when it's not in balance it can be exhausting and can lead to anger, exhaustion and frustration. So whenever you give, make sure you have enough to give. You can't pour from an empty cup, right? I'm going to explain how giving causes happiness but can also feel heavy when it's not received back in another form.

You' might have heard that time is the most expensive thing we can give to someone because we can't buy it, nor can we bring it back. When we spend our time with people we love, giving them a beautiful gift. It's the gift of our presence. We enjoy being with them and they feel the same. We know how precious time is, so we indulge every moment and we love to see how much they enjoy our presence. However, there are situations in our lives when giving our time to someone can be very draining. We all know the saying: 'I'm just wasting my time with you.' By wasting our time, we mean giving our energy that goes to someone who only receives and we don't get any form of their energy back. Giving and receiving is an energy exchange that has to be in balance. If we feel we give more than we receive, with time our body energy might decrease and we find ourselves sad, exhausted or angry because eventually we have less energy than we had before, which creates a bad mood and negative emotions.

When we give we have two reasons to do so: The first one is voluntary; we give because we want to or we feel we need to give. Our instincts want to give (for example charity work), so we consciously decide to give our energy to someone regardless of whether they give anything back.

The second one is with an intention, when we know our energy is mutual with the person or the thing and we know we get our energy back in another form, for example a relationship. It works fifty-fifty. We give a massage to our partner and the next day they give a massage to us or bring us some surprise gift. It can be anything. Basically, we know our energy is appreciated in any form.

CHAPTER TWENTY-ONE

DON'T GIVE A FUCK, DARLING

That would also be my honest advice for happiness. Sometimes we get carried away with the constant avalanches of thoughts about what people think of us. When we really care about what others think, we steal our own happiness from ourselves because the idea of others criticising, gossiping or pointing at our weak spots affects our lives and destroys our happiness. For instance, before we go out and decide to wear something really sexy for the first time, we often think whether people will be laughing at us or how they'll be looking at us or the worst and most absurd scenario: what they will think of us!

Firstly, what other people think is made up by us in our own mind. In other words, people are our mirrors, so what we think of ourselves, people 'think' of us. In most cases of worrying what people think, we create dramas in our own head. Basically, others 'judge' us exactly the same as we judge ourselves.

Secondly, ninety-nine per cent of the dramas we create never happen. From my own experience, I can tell you that almost every time when I worried about what people would do to me and say to me, I was pleasantly surprised because it ended up completely different and, very often, much better than I thought it would.

Thirdly, worrying about 'haters' and what they think of us takes a lot of time out of our day and our precious moments. So, next time people's thoughts matter to you, imagine grabbing the thought and chucking it like a piece of paper in the bin. It will no longer matter to you and, as a reward, you'll get peace. It will be peace of your own mind, focusing on what is really important, which is what YOU think about yourself and how YOU feel.

Being comfortable and confident with who you are will give you much more freedom and save you the wasted time you'd spend on thinking what others think of you, because other voices and anything around you won't matter any more.

Find out more about being at one with yourself and staying in your inner peace in the next chapter.

CHAPTER TWENTY-TWO

INNER PEACE

I used to be stressed when I was late for my dentist appointment, late for other things, felt under pressure because other people were looking at me at the restaurant (simply because my first thought was to wonder why they were looking at me, what was 'wrong' with me, even though I felt great and beautiful). I was worried what people thought of me, but then I read the Dalai Lama's quote: 'Don't let the behaviour of others destroy your inner peace', and it really moved me.

It doesn't matter what is going on around us, we should still stay the same within. Before I perform or go to any big event where I know lots of people will be looking at me (it can be my stage performing in clubs or festivals, hosting, modelling, public speaking), I tend to get nervous because I imagine their faces and their reactions, along with my face and my reactions. I get completely thrown by nothing but my own thoughts. I've tried to work on it, and I found a great practice. Before any event I know is usually stressful or high-class or pretentious, or it's all about looks and the atmosphere is just not very raw, real and happy, I close my eyes and imagine myself all natural without fancy clothes, make-up, and jewellery. I see myself in nature (sometimes it's my favourite beach in Sydney, sometimes it's my childhood memory in the forest in the middle of nowhere and me walking barefoot in the meadow right next to the forest) and sometimes I imagine myself in the arms of my grandma, who means kindness, love and safety to me. In both memories I feel happy; I'm being myself, in peace, being the raw, real me. I really imagine myself there as I am living that moment again.

Suddenly, all the pressure and nervousness disappears and I stand only with myself in that feeling, and I know there is no one else around me. I feel in peace, certain about who I am, honest with who I am and how I want to feel. It's like my little meditation before any event, or even a work interview; at any time my peace might be interrupted by thoughts full of fear and prejudices.

One morning I found out I had only £40 in my account for the next three weeks. I felt stressed, and while I was walking from my house to the train station I got carried away by all the worrying about money and didn't even realise it was a beautiful, sunny day. The sky was blue, there were sunbeams on my face and I stopped for a moment, almost shocked, realising I didn't see or feel the beauty around me. I completely stopped perceiving what was going on around me because I was so overwhelmed about what was happening in my own world.

That moment, I decided I wouldn't let my fear, worries or any thoughts in general destroy my inner peace, stop me from experiencing beautiful things around me or take me away from the present moment. So, when I go through situations like this, I close my eyes, see no one around me, complete darkness, then I transfer myself into the feeling of the biggest peace possible. I am there, I experience it; I take a few deep breaths, get calm, smile and then open my eyes, feeling so different and much more peaceful. You can do the same, or you can find your own way to keep your inner peace at any time you feel shattered, stressed or worried. In general, I've found that taking five to ten deep breaths and focusing on breathing works for most people. In that time, your stress level drops, your heartbeat slows and you are connected with your own breath. You will reach your inner peace very quickly.

CHAPTER TWENTY-THREE

THE INFLUENCE OF OTHERS ON OUR HAPPINESS

What others think is not important. If there is a person in your life that tells you too often what you should do, tell them: 'Thank you for your opinion, I really appreciate that. But from now on, I want to hear what you think only when I ask, thank you for your understanding.'

Remember, there is a difference between being nice and sweet and saying yes to everyone, and being nice but knowing when you need to stop things that steal your energy, confidence, freedom etc. There are so many nice ways to say: 'Enough.' Saying 'enough' to people you don't need any more is not a sign of selfishness; it is a beautiful way to express your confidence, strong character, so you are happy you can live freely without holding bad energy and worrying what others tell you.

Naturally, we want to flow through life with ease and live with everyone around us in harmony. It is the good, positive, fresh energy that attracts you to others. It's the happy postman you see every day; you don't have to know anything about his life, but there is something that creates the reason you are so happy to see him. The something is the vibe, energy, sometimes I call it aura. This has been proved in my life; it really exists and really works.

For example, I was introduced to a girl with a gorgeous smile one night. We started to talk about really common things such as where we were from, what we were doing, where we used to go for a swim etc. We smiled through the whole conversation. We had just met each other, but we knew there was a huge magic (vibes, energy, aura) connecting us. It was almost like a magnet, a really addictive magnet. It was a feeling of friendship, honesty, and it felt so good to hang out with her. I haven't spoken with her since then, but I know if I see her even in ten years, it will look like we saw each other just recently, with a pure feeling of a friendly trust again.

You love to spend your time with people who uplift you, right? You can tell if you feel lighter or heavier after seeing your friends (more about friendship in my next chapter). This is an important one. You call them friends because you've known them since kindergarten. You often see them just because of this 'we've been friends forever' friendship. You like them and they like you, but your soul feels that it isn't right. You feel heavier because there is not the energy exchange I mentioned earlier.

A cool example of an energy exchange is a deer in forest that eats grass and then eliminates it, providing a good quality compost for the new grass that is about to grow, which will be eaten again and again and again. It's a really simple and silly example, but can you see? This is the energy exchange in nature. This is how it's been working for ages. And this is how relationships between us humans work too: I give you something = you receive it, you give something = I receive something from you. This is how the world works. This is how the energy works in my world.

After I got from Australia back to the Czechia, I spent weeks just by myself and only my parents and my brother. I wouldn't leave the house if I didn't have to. I even told them to keep it a secret that I was back because everyone would've been so excited to see me immediately.

There were a few reasons I spent my time at home; I felt very creative, so I just wanted to stay in my bedroom and create my crafts and paint and write. Also, I had undertaken laser surgery for my eyes, so I was limited a bit. But, mostly, I came back to my parents' house wiser. I knew I could choose who I was going to see and who not. I had a best friend, I used to hang out with her all my childhood, and we have so many beautiful memories together. However, after my arrival, I didn't even text her; I just didn't feel like seeing her. I texted her brother instead because we'd been texting each other and he needed me and I needed him, and we are both artists and love each other's company. His energy is mutual, whereas with her I felt like I was the giver; I was the one who made the happy atmosphere and gave all the advice and was exhausted by complaining and talking about other people.

I took a deep breath in and said to myself: 'I choose people who give me what I deserve.' I've understood some people are only a beautiful phase, short or long, and we are not obligated to see them for the rest of our lives if we don't feel the same any more. It might seem cruel and selfish, and the people can miss you, but you know you follow the happy path in your life. Again, it's your life, your happiness, and this is all that matters.

Know your energy needs and limits, find your 'energy mates' and don't worry, the universe will send to them the right people to cross their paths and connect with the right energy, and maybe it's gonna be fifty-fifty this time.

CHAPTER TWENTY-FOUR

FRIENDS

Having friends is such a blessing. The other day I was thinking about the word 'friend'. As I was repeating the word over and over again, I couldn't stop being amazed how special this word/the person is. A friend is someone who deserves to wear this label. It's someone who's been in my life for some time, who I can trust, and they can trust me. Being a friend is a mutual bond; it is loving, respecting, helping, caring for each other, making each other happy. A friend makes us laugh. We can go on adventures with them, we can share our secrets, we cry on their shoulders, we can be vulnerable and sensitive and truly authentic to ourselves without hiding anything, and yet they still love us not for how we look but who we really are on the inside. They want to spend some time with us because they love our company.

I use the word 'friends' for people I met just once, or I just know them from a party or work. They're not close to me and I wouldn't probably share my secrets with them, but we call each other friends just because we know each other from somewhere and had a good time. And then I use the word friends for amazing, special, beloved people so close to me that I love them as my family and would do anything for them. These people somehow showed up in my heart and I never forget them, even when they're gone or live in a different country or have passed away. They are there for me when I need help, they make me laugh, they inspire me and make my life less lonely.

Often I imagine how it would be if I was the only one on the planet. I love being alone, in my own environment, peace, being by myself, writing, reading, having fun, listening to music all by myself. I love being by myself most of the time, but then there are moments I need someone because my life feels empty and I need company. That someone is a friend! We can see each other, hug each other, have a nice conversation together, go dancing. To me having a friend is being grateful for a human connection and making the most of it.

I'm grateful for every friendship I've had. It reflects on my own life. It teaches me how to behave and how not to behave. People inspire me, motivate me, sometimes show me the sides I don't like and how I don't want to become, but they definitely affect the way I live.

FRIENDS> Fabulous Reason I Extremely Nourish Dear Someone

CHAPTER TWENTY-FIVE

THE MAGIC IN YOU

You know you have something special, right? You don't know what it is, but you know you have it. People call it charisma, energy, personality, the X factor, sparkle, etc. I will call it magic. It is this indescribable part of you that makes your personality complete, actually makes your personality different to anyone else. You might get compliments on your magic, you might get admiration for your magic and, most of all, you get people who want that magic too. They are attracted to your magic so much that they want to spend all the time they have with you. They are intrigued by your magic and want to find out more about it.

From my own experience, people who really like my magic and want to get to know me are often those whose magic I like too, and eventually we become good friends. The magic in you is visible and it's catchy.

If you can put your finger on your magic and you know what it is that makes you so special, work with that. Try to show it to everyone, and see it as your big strength and quality. That's how you'll find your tribe in the world and get connections you always dreamt of.

CHAPTER TWENTY-SIX

ACCEPT AND BE ACCEPTED

Those who have been through bullying or people laughing at them or pointing at them will definitely understand. As a gay boy in the village (at that time, maybe the only one) I was always a centre of attention because I was different (they often called me 'the four per cent one'). I was different in the way I was dressing (pink shoes I got from my cousin were a big shock for my teachers), the way I was speaking (for other ten-year-old kids I was too gay, and that wasn't good), the way I was presenting myself (they called it girly moves). I was different, so I was seen, which I always wanted anyway, but sometimes I wanted to be like the other boys and laugh with them. Sometimes I cried, sometimes I wanted to hide my true identity, sometimes I wanted to kill myself, sometimes I just wanted to be like others, but I never stopped being strong.

With time (almost ten years), I slowly started loving myself and being comfortable with who I was. I embraced who I was, maybe because I moved to Australia and I met more like-minded people who had the same interests or even a similar story to me. I stopped trying to be like someone else. I simply accepted myself for who I was. It was when I was nineteen. I remember. With my 'coming out' came confidence and a completely new me who believed in myself and, this is important, started seeing everyone as beautiful human beings and accepting them. It wasn't too early, it wasn't too late. It was just the right timing.

I wrote this chapter before I knew I was transgender. I decided to keep it here even though it's not really comfortable to me right now as it's still fresh, but it's my history and my truth, so I'm going to keep it here. Anyway, I'm going to share my second coming out in one life here too, because it did take another acceptance. The beginnings of my trans coming out weren't as hard as announcing I was gay, but it was harder for myself. With being gay, it took me years to accept it, but I knew it was truth. With being trans, I accepted it immediately but I still wasn't sure, as to me it was completely new and a much different feeling to my sexual orientation.

Anyway, within a few months, I found myself again, accepted that and told everyone. I found a strong woman in me and, since then, I've been fighting for equality for everyone. I want everyone to know they are accepted. I want to show you how my life significantly changed after accepting everything. Because I wasn't always accepted for who I was as I was the minority (minority means someone who is different compared with most), I know how it feels, and so whenever I see the minority in the streets (basically anyone who is different to others, or brave enough to leave their house despite being different, being who they are), I give them a high five or I scream 'yaaaaass' at them, just to show them they're not alone and they're doing great.

Mainly I have 'my gay boys' in mind, because this is the closest topic of acceptance to me, and that's what I imagine when I say acceptance. Boys who wear make-up, dress against society's norms, express themselves as they want to, take their persona to the next level. That's how I used to do it, and I loved it. It takes balls to do this and be rebellious, and I feel so much for these boys who have been despised and now want to show who they are and want to scream how proud they are and want to shine. Also my 'trans sisters' who face laughter, the same questions every day, mental issues, refusal, falling confidence, fear of facing people face to face, but are still standing tall and strong because they will never change, and sometimes even can't change, who they are.

Also, anyone who is from a different cultural or religious background, who seems to be more vulnerable than their mates, who is rejected for their look, fashion sense, style, anyone who has a different body shape to others, a different face shape, a different height or talks slower. I want to let them know they're not alone, that they are beautiful and they are accepted. By accepting others, you acknowledge their individuality, their inner and outer beauty, their expression, their existence! Being not always accepted by others opens your eyes and heart. You become more compassionate and caring because you've been in their shoes before.

CHAPTER TWENTY-SEVEN

KINDNESS

'There are no strangers. Only friends you haven't yet met.'
~William Butler Yeats~

Everyone is my friend. I live like that. If there is a stranger that needs help, I imagine it's my family member or a friend that needs my help. If there are people trying to approach you and have a conversation, maybe give them a chance, maybe they are interested to work with you on their project, maybe they just admire your beauty or maybe they are your future friends. There is no need to judge or to be cold.

Kindness is a great guide to be nice to everyone around you, to treat everyone equally. When we are kind to strangers around us, we know that anytime we come to a new environment, we'll be welcomed with kindness and treated with respect too. We don't have to fear people; we are all cousins, we are all family, we are all one.

Sometimes I hear the saying: 'You made my day.' Isn't it a wonderful way to express your reaction to a certain experience and show them your grateful, happy smile? You both leave satisfied, you both know you've left a nice memory in each other's hearts. This is one kind of kindness. You are kind to someone for a reason. You want to put energy and effort (I know in cold winter mornings it can be hard to be bubbly, smiley and energetic) into the act of kindness because you feel you have the gift to give all of you today, and in return you might get kindness from another person who wants to explore the warm feeling in their hearts too.

I try to treat everyone the same, even if they're not kind to me. I need to be the strong one and show them the way, show them how kindness is done. I really believe that kindness is the key. I believe with kindness we can have smooth relationships, deeper connections and a more meaningful life, because with our 'teaching kindness' we can learn from others. We will be able to see how they become better versions of themselves, how they start helping others, how they start to acknowledge other's actions and behaviours. Kindness can improve the 'human Wi-Fi of the world,' as I call connections between each other, because we are all connected to someone through someone. So the more often we use kindness in our daily routine, the stronger the 'human Wi-Fi signal' we will create on the planet and the happier our life will be. Eventually, kindness will be a part of every day because it will become completely natural to you.

That is how I see kindness, and how I would like other humans to treat me and everyone else. That is one of the biggest dreams in my life. To get a bit closer towards my dreams, I need to be the one who takes the first step, I really want to live in peace and a safe world in general. I know I am the world I create, therefore any actions I take and any situations I find myself in must be acts of kindness without bad intentions, anger, spite, dishonesty, malice or disrespect.

CHAPTER TWENTY-EIGHT

SHARING

We live in a great time when we can constantly be updated and see what the rest of the world is doing. We can video-call with our friends who live on the other side of the planet, we can follow everyone, and everyone can follow us. And this is a great opportunity to share your life!

If you share your dreams, your desires, hobbies, passions, people see that and they know what your dream is, what your talent is, and they might find someone who can help you get where you want to be. They can be a great intermediary between the vision and the action. I really love this age because I can meet people for the first time but, because they know me already from social media, they know what topic to talk about or they know my work and my story without me introducing it and explaining anything. For example, I met a couple in the city, and they go: 'Hey, we know you. We just checked your Insta account this morning, we loved your videos.' They know who I am, they know that I share my deep feelings and thoughts and they know what level of conversation they can expect from me. Also, it feels great and I'm really comfortable; I know I can be myself and speak my truth without worrying if they understand me, because I'm understood already.

So take the chance and share, share, share everything you love, your thoughts and opinions. Speak your truth, because somewhere out there is your tribe. It can be a person from a different continent who has the same story as you and you start chatting. It can be a TV producer who can find you so amazing and gifted and can be your biggest fan, and you might start your own TV show. If there is anything you can share, do it 100 per cent and often, and make sure you're not putting it out there just face to face and online but also to the universe!... so it becomes manifesting too.

CHAPTER TWENTY-NINE

MANIFESTING

I really believe in my own power, and you can too. You can share your dreams in your prayers or with your family and friends, even on social media, as people can sometimes stick to your manifesting, and they manifest together with you when you share that dream or idea with them. I share all my desires, my dreams; I see this as a form of manifesting and making my dreams come true, because everything I say and write down can become reality (sometimes I get so paranoid with typing on my phone and even funny messages to my friends, such as: 'We're gonna be forever single', or 'I wanna die right now'. I delete them before I send them because, even though it's meant to be an exaggerated joke, I believe whatever I put out is vibrating to the universe and I'll get it back.

Whatever I put out there, I manifest it, and the more people see it, the more powerful my manifesting will be. So, the more you share your desires with others, the more powerful your wish will be, and it can come true even faster.

We get what we want. We get what we believe in. If you still don't believe in it, think of Wi-Fi. You search for some information on the internet and you get it back in a second. You know it's because of the Wi-Fi and its signal and vibrations. You can't see the Wi-Fi signal, but you know it exists because you see the result immediately. It's the same with your thoughts and manifesting; your desires vibrate to the source and they go back to you as an answer to the request you've sent and, as a result of the successful connection, you receive what you've asked for.

Manifesting is real and, the older I get, the more my dreams become reality and I just accept all of it, while doing 'woooow', as everything seems so simple and logical when we get what we've been manifesting, yet so difficult while we're manifesting.

CHAPTER THIRTY

THE WORLD OUTSIDE

I am happy because I create the happiness in myself, in my own world, but I am also happy because of the people around me. People have such a big impact on our lives. From my experience, they have a big impact on my mood. Sometimes I get up and I'm not the shiny happy Pavie I usually am, but there can be a stranger in the shop or a barista or my close friend, or anyone that day, and they smile at me in such a nice and warm way, or they give me a compliment and I start to smile too. Or I'm crossing the road, feeling down, insecure and not attractive at that moment, and the guy sitting outside a coffee shop says: 'Hello beautiful, what's your name, gorgeous?' Suddenly he makes me happier and more confident.

I'm so grateful for these people; because of them, I don't spend the rest of the day in a miserable mood, or a mood I can't even put finger on, and I leave them uplifted and happier.

We are made of thoughts. You are created of your thoughts and the thoughts of everything you've ever heard and read. These thoughts can make you feel a certain way. You are responsible for the people you let into your life and everything you surround yourself with. You can filter your toxic thoughts from the good ones that you want in your life. Who made an impact on your thoughts today? Who did you see today? What did they tell you? Did you hear more gossip or beautiful stories about interesting people? Did you read a motivational article? Did you listen to a podcast that inspired and made you feel on top of the world?

The world outside can make you cry and smile at the same time. Once you realise the reality around you is actually your reality and everything that is happening to you is actually happening in your thoughts, you'll be the director of your movie. You'll be the one in charge, filtering all the toxic shit that doesn't help you at all, makes you unhappy, demotivated and sad.

CHAPTER THIRTY-ONE

FEED FROM YOUR FEED

W e are responsible for everything we feed our body with. We know we need to eat healthy food and exercise and live in balance to live a good-quality life.

We don't feed only our bodies, though; we also feed our brain and soul with all the information we receive through our entire life. You've probably heard the saying 'You are what you eat'. For me, this isn't only about healthy diet and food in general; this saying involves anything I receive in my body and mind, whether it's food, drinks, books, news, articles, travelling, observing.

As we can choose what we put in our bodies, we can also choose what we read, what we watch and what we 'put in' our brain which receives all the information. I really believe we become the person we want to be regardless of our origin, culture, family beliefs, education when we were kids. We can become the best versions of ourselves step by step, shaping our mind and our core beliefs. We can become a completely new person and start living a new life by changing our habits, being mindful and willing to change.

There are so many studies showing people's health being changed by only the power of their mind. Their pain disappeared after a placebo pill which basically was just some white powder without any effect, only because their body decided to heal itself, 'knowing' it has the cure needed to be pain-free. Our mind works the same; once we change our habits, beliefs, affirmations, the environment, we can become a completely whole new person regardless our past experience. Let's say we start meditating, doing yoga or jogging; we are likely to be more relaxed, calm and handle stressful or challenging situations with ease and a calm mind. If we start reading positive things and surround ourselves with positive people, we are more likely to complain less and be less negative. If we surround ourselves with successful people, guess what? Our brain starts to think like successful people do.

So now we know we have the power to choose what information to absorb and how our environment and surroundings shape us.

We are the generation of technology and social media. We use our phones all day, every day. We wake up and scroll down our Instagram and Facebook and some days it is the first information we receive before our day begins. It is the way we start the day, even before we eat or go to the toilet. We can choose who and what we follow; it is our choice to wake up and see pictures that can make us feel a certain way. Maybe the edited pictures of models can make us feel less beautiful or like we are not successful enough because we don't have the yacht like that guy from our feed. We see tens of our friends smiling while we woke up sad and demotivated, and sometimes we tend to compare our lives with theirs, so it can make us feel even more sad, or we feel we are not successful enough because the girl who is the same age has over five million followers and you only have 500. Or we think we live in a dangerous and chaotic word because you are hit by violent, aggressive and negative posts.

If none of these posts change your mood, make you feel differently or make you compare your life to others, fine, keep following what you've been following.

We scroll through hundreds of pictures and posts that make us feel some way. Our brain processes this information and we start our day this way. Remember, you can choose who you follow and what is the first thing you read in the morning. Is it inspiring quotes, positive affirmations, peaceful pictures of nature, happy, positive posts? Or is it gossip from Hollywood, posts putting people down, demotivating jokes or your complaining classmate from high school (who you haven't seen for ten years, but you know he spilled his coffee in the morning and he's very angry now)? What do you follow and how does it make you feel? Do you really care about those people? Do you really want to see what a stranger on the other side of the world has just eaten? Are you really obsessed with that celebrity? Have these things become a part of your everyday life, or can you pause and think if you really need to see that?

Scrolling is definitely one of the most common ways we feed our mind nowadays. We should take advantage of the fact we have access to all the information in the world and work out how we can benefit from it, how to use it to learn, grow, thrive, get inspired and help ourselves and others.

It is the same with the news. I really believe we live in the world that we decide to. Our beliefs are influenced by the beliefs of others, our reality is influenced by people around us, our perspective is influenced by books we read and podcasts we listen to, our thoughts are influenced by anything that crosses our path. Anything. This is the important word. Whether we like it or not, we absorb anything that is happening to us through the day. When we are conscious enough and can think about what information we receive during the day, we realise we don't want to absorb everything that we see; we want to read something different or happier that will make us feel how we want to feel, or information that will help, educate or inspire us.

CHAPTER THIRTY-TWO

DON'T WATCH NEWS

When I was at my boarding school, I used to watch news every day. Every night at 7:30pm I went to the living room and turned the TV on. I wanted to know what important events had happened that day, to expand my horizons and stay updated with the general knowledge that 'everyone should have'. Next day, when the teacher asked our class about the news from the previous night, I always knew. I still don't know why I wanted to know everything. Maybe I just wanted to impress my teacher and be a good student? Maybe I thought it was super-important to know what the rest of the world was doing?

When I moved to Sydney, I had no TV and I didn't read any news, not even the Czech news. I had no clue what was going on in the country I was living in or the rest of the world. Eventually I realised I didn't need any information from the news to be smarter or to have a more meaningful life. A few years later, I know that media knowledge doesn't define your smartness or education. If we want more knowledge, if we have the desire to get those question marks in our heads answered, if we want to learn something new, we can choose what information we are going to feed our mind and soul with.

If you haven't noticed already, most of the news is full of fear, violence and negativity, and I have decided that this is not what I want to feed my mind with. We all are responsible for information we absorb. We can choose what we see on TV and how it leaves us feeling. We can choose who we

follow on social media and what picture or celebrity quote will be stuck in our heads the whole day. We can choose what book we read. We all have some topics we want to know more about. Education is not sitting in the classroom our whole childhood and then becoming adult, thinking we've made it and are ready to live our lives. Education is seeking the truth, searching for the information we want to know more deeply, it's filling up our brains with joy, passion, meaning and purpose to find out why we are here. So, instead of the half an hour I would spend on watching TV, I feed my soul as I want to, with anything that moves me forward and nourishes my mind.

Nowadays most of the news come from social media anyway, so we don't really have the choice to escape the most important world events, tragedies, politics, natural disasters, social crises etc. All we can do is keep scrolling down instead of opening the news up when you know it's about a topic you aren't really related to, or you don't care, or you don't want to hear the negativity. It is not selfish to not want to know how many people have died today, to carry the pain of the rest of the world, to go to sleep without a fear of terrorist attacks, to keep yourself in a happy mood because your mind thinks we live in a safe world.

I'm definitely not a selfish, cold or cruel person for not watching the news. I do care about the world, especially the environment, and if there are things I can change then I do it. If there are things I cannot change, I let them go, don't think about them any more, don't get upset or angry. If there is any action needed, or event or charity, and I can and want to take the necessary step to help someone or make the world a happier place with my little help or donation, I do it. We definitely can change the world, but firstly we need to take the first little right step in our lives because as you know it counts.

CHAPTER THIRTY-THREE

ASK

If you want to know the answer, ask! As they say, the answer is always no if you don't ask.

I went home from visiting my friend in Vienna. On the bus, I realised I left my phone charger and adapter in my friend's room and I needed it. I wanted him to send my stuff to me. I knew he was really busy and didn't know Vienna properly to go to the post office, but in my head there was a thought: 'If I ask, he can say yes or no, easy. If he says no, I'll be in the same situation as now and I'll need to buy my things again. If he says yes, I'll get the charger back without paying anything and I'll be so happy.' Two simple choices. So I asked and I got my phone charger with the adaptor in my mailbox within a week. I was so proud of myself; I didn't even know what I was afraid of. I know, it's a bit nerve-racking to ask for a favour, but if you ask, there is a very satisfying feeling afterwards, and you're not asking yourself: 'What if I'd asked?' Whether it's asking your friend for £10, asking for a lighter or trying to understand the story your friend has explained three times already, asking is important. However stupid you might seem or however silly the question can sound to you, if you want to have the answer and you know what to ask, do it. Always from today. DO. IT!

If there is any question in your head during the day, always try to have it answered before you go to sleep. Wisdom is a beautiful thing and if there is anything you'd like to know or anything in your field you could educate yourself on, go for it!

I just remembered this quote: 'If you ask now you might look stupid, if you don't ask at all, you're gonna be stupid for the rest of your life.' This quote always encourages me to ask, to wonder, to be the best version of myself I can possibly be.

CHAPTER THIRTY-FOUR

RELEASE THE TENSION/
THE POWER OF THE WORD

You have the power to transform negative energy into a new, positive one. Are you surrounded by negative people, negative news or even negative members of your family? Do you love being positive and avoid anything that's negative? Do you have just enough of all the negative bullshit around you? Well, you might've been seeking help here, but you don't know one thing: You can help yourself. You are the one who decides whether you accept everything that's happening around you, and you can also change how to react to it. Your mind is an amazing tool, it can do anything! And you can control that! You can choose how you'll react to some negative information.

Imagine there's your friend telling you gossip and news about someone's sadness, and he/she really loves talking about negativity and the problems of others, and you've just had enough. Well, if you're really sick of them, you always have the choice to stop hanging out with the people. But, in some cases, you'll really like the person and won't want to stop talking to them just because they are excited about a catastrophe in the newspapers, even though it can seem bizarre. So you can either tell them you'd prefer to talk about your lives, happiness, plans, favourite things, basically anything that wouldn't be as negative. Or you can absorb all the information and don't hold it, but release it! Oh yes you can.

Try to picture this: you have a really negative day; you hear negative info on the radio, someone was shouting at you from the car, your mate was mad at you, you can be mad even at yourself because you haven't done some work you were planning to do. And now you're going home to see your family for dinner, and now this is the important moment. You have the power to change the world! (This is the phrase you've been hearing for so long, and never had a clue how you can do it.)

You have two options:

a) You can feel the anger, temper and rage inside you, but you are mindful. You take a few deep breaths, connect with yourself and you go home and start talking about the problems that happened to you with your head calm and mindful, asking for a solution, staying true to finding a solution.

b) You can hold your anger, trying to get over it/forget it as quickly as you can (cigarettes for stress, a glass of red to calm you down) instead of being honest and having a conversation with yourself about how you're feeling. You don't mention your problems to anyone but, because you're so mad at everything, you start being mad at your family too. This is where the power of your words lie. Ask yourself: What's the matter? How am I feeling about it? What am I going to do with it? What action am I going to take?

CHAPTER THIRTY-FIVE

THE POWER OF YOU

You are amazing! You already know it, right? And do you know you have the power to change people's mood? If you want to make a happy world (once it's all good in your own happy world) you need to radiate happiness. The whole world; that is all up to you.

Once I was going to buy a drink at a kiosk. When I was approaching the bar, the waitress was obviously fed up with something. She asked me: 'Hey, what would you like?' with a very bored and disgusted tone of voice and the look of her face. In that moment, I decided to be the one who will change the future and her day, and the energy there in general. I said: 'Hi, how are you today?' with a very cheerful attitude and a big smile. She said: 'Good, good'. Then I was choosing a drink and asking her about some beers and brands. My tone of voice was really curious, and I must've looked so interested asking her about the taste and flavour of the drinks.

The truth is I was interested, but I wanted more to talk to her as long as I could and give her as much positive energy as I could. I just wanted to. She also could express her bartender skills and talk about the beverages a bit more. You can see the sparkles in people's eyes when they're explaining something and you're listening to them, looking curious and amazed. They're happy that you're interested and they can talk about what they like even more passionately. I don't know if the girl was passionate about her job, but I got what I wanted: I got a delicious drink I hadn't tried before, and I got her smile when I was saying bye. She became a completely different person with her smile, suddenly so kind and open and I knew it was because of the 'Pavie magic' I gave her. On my way back, I popped in again, and she was already smiling and greeting me as if I was her really good friend. That night I fell asleep knowing I made someone's day brighter. If you think you have this skill to make people feel better after you leave them, if you know you love making strangers happier, then do it as often as you can. The world needs people like us. This is how we change the world. And this is what makes us happy; the feeling of making others happy.

There is a continuing of this story. It doesn't always end only with a happy mood for them or a great feeling and happiness for you. Imagine people's thrill and happiness when they, for example, finish work and go home. They feel good, right? They feel light and happy because they can relax or eat their favourite food. If you make their day, they're definitely going to share it with someone else because, when we are impressed or astonished by a nice experience, we want to tell our partner at home or our best friend. This is the second part of sprinkling your inner power. The fact people share their happy experience will make other people in their lives happy. The more people they'll tell about it, the more people will have a happy experience in their head too. Think of this girl from my story who is at home, she tells her friend about this girl who made her day (the more you amaze people, the more they'll be sharing the experience). Then she tells her mum and dad, and maybe five of her friends at school the next day. That means she shared SOMETHING happy with eight people. Not only do they believe a bit more that the world is full of beautiful people, they're also inspired to do the same to others. They also want to be amazing and make someone else's day. These eight people have a thought of happiness in their mind. Just because of me, because I put in the effort (actually I didn't, it was a pleasure) and started to talk to this girl. Really think about the power of you.

Visualise our planet where everyone is a lightbulb; instead of people walking around you, you see walking lightbulbs. Every day each bulb would wake up turned off, with no light. Once a bulb helps another (gives a compliment, gives it positive energy, makes it happier in some way) both bulbs would light up. We are the bulbs all connected with each other and we can choose if we want to live in the darkness or shine and spread light around us.

Also, you have the power to make people create an opinion of themselves. You know how? If you tell them that they're useless, they have no sense of humour, they're selfish or they're stupid, they're gonna think about that for sure. The more they think about it, the more they're gonna believe it. I know they can choose whether they accept or not, but why would you tell them this? You know you have this gift to make people feel in a certain way, so why would you make them feel sad and down? You can tell them something which is gonna make them feel happy, uplifted and important. If you tell your friend that he or she is a beautiful human being, they will be more than happy to accept your compliment and, eventually, they'll accept that and start to believe that they really are beautiful and amazing or however you choose to call them. And you've certainly experienced the feeling of happiness after you make someone else happy. It's such a beautiful feeling.

CHAPTER THIRTY-SIX

SAY WHAT YOU FEEL

L ive every day like it's your last. Say what you want to say at every moment. Say what just feels good to YOU. When you answer, don't try to please anyone else, not even people who are in a higher social or working position, because even those people want to hear you, your inner truth, your raw human experience. Anyway, people are sick of those clichéd answers, lies and fake smiles which often hide anger and sadness. Once you live your life, you live for yourself, you live how you want, doing whatever suits you and whatever feels good to you, right?

For example, I came back to Czechia from Sydney after three years. I was on one dating app, chatting to a boy, starting my conversation in English, which is not the first language there. After a few minutes we discussed where we were from. I said Sydney but born in Czechia because I really did feel Australian in my heart. After living in Sydney, I felt the Australian culture, lifestyle, the whole experience remained in me. When he found out I'd been out of the country for only three years, he asked me whether I could chat in Czech and I said yes, but I'd prefer English because it was easier and more comfortable for me. He didn't understand it, so he stopped talking to me because I was 'weird'.

But that's not the point. The point is I said what I wanted and how I felt. When I looked back after a month, I was happy I did so because we never met, never talked again and I was proud of myself that this boy I took very seriously didn't win over my feelings and my truth that moment.

Whatever circumstances you might have in your life, always say what is right for you and what feels right to you regardless of the rejection you might suffer. This is freedom.

CHAPTER THIRTY-SEVEN

LOVE

I've been hearing people saying that love is the most important thing in our lives. I never really understood it. I thought it was just a cliché; I even thought people were making it up because I never loved, never had a partner and never celebrated Valentine's Day. To me, this was the love I was supposed to feel. I didn't know love was everything around me, or realise the time and energy of my parents was love too.

One day, I got it. I am love. I've been loving all my life. It started early when I was a kid. I loved to cuddle with my parents before I fell asleep; it was a strong bond, and I never wanted them to leave and always wanted to hear more and more stories from childhood. That was love. I was protecting (sometimes overprotecting) my younger brother. When my parents were gone, we watched the movies and I felt like I was his guardian angel. That was love. Every year when the school year finished, I wanted to collect money to buy my teachers a beautiful present to show them how much I loved them and appreciated their energy. I wanted to make sure the teacher felt my compassion and my huge 'thank you' smile. That was love.

Through my adolescent years, I often went to enjoy nature after school. I would run on the top of the hill and, with a tomato, fresh bread and cheese, enjoy the view, the grass and the sky. I perfectly remember the temperature, the smell of the air, the freedom I felt. (I'm actually crying with nostalgia right now, there is so much beauty in these memories). My grandpa and my mum showed me all my childhood the relationship to nature. I've always found freedom and peace there. I always knew she (nature) was my home; she could always hear me out and help me to find my inner balance, in the woods or meadows. That was love.

I love to share my beautiful moments. When I was living in Australia I called my grandma once a week and told her about all the beautiful things I saw, often about flowers or any nature-related things. I told her how I felt in this and that place, and shared my joy of life with her. Even when my parents came to Sydney to visit me, I was twenty but I would still drag them to show them my favourite streets, even though they had to rush to the airport. I showed them where I used to go for a run every day, how I felt there, what I loved about that house on the corner, and I just wanted to see their faces. That moment when they listened to my stories about the beauty of my everyday life, that moment they were part of my amazing experience, that moment of their understanding, that moment of my sharing – this was love too.

We are made of love. We were created by the Universe/Divine/Source/Creator who made us in perfect love and harmony with the Universe. Our parents may not have made us in love but our Creator loves us and there are no mistakes. The love we have never disappears, never goes away, never leaves us. We have the love and we as human beings need to love and be loved, whether it's a relationship, romantic love, platonic love, secret love, love for your favourite singer, love of animals, love to yourself, love in books, love in movies, love in songs etc.

The older I am, the fuller of love I am. I feel so much love inside of me that I just want to love all day. I just want to walk through my house, almost dancing, and I want to hug and kiss all my family members and dearest friends any time I pass them. I just want to make others feel good and loved because today I know what love means and how love looks, and I know I can love. We all can. We all have the big bright light within us. By being kind, showing our compassion, loving our lives, sharing the beauty of our lives with others, we all contribute to this energy that connects all life forms in the universe, and this force is unstoppable.

CHAPTER THIRTY-EIGHT

MY THEORY

I love sharing happiness and positive energy. If I know I have the power to share love, I share that in all its forms. I try to share positivity in every conversation I have in a day. That means the person, after meeting me, feels happier and full of positive energy because I gave them a positive experience. Do you believe in positive energy? Do you love being happy and do you want to share happiness around you too? If you meet twenty people a day and tell them anything with a positive intention, you're going to have a beautiful day, because those people will share their experience around and you're going to feel great that you could make the world a more positive place.

For example, someone asked me if I'd tried bikram yoga and what my opinion was about it. I had two choices. (And, actually, you always do. You can always decide whether you are going to share a positive or negative experience or opinion). I went for the positive one. I could have said: 'It's too hot, I felt dizzy, it's too long and every class is the same.' But I said: 'It's amazing, definitely give a try, I gained a kilo of lean muscle in one month and lost two per cent of my body fat, got more flexible and felt amazing after every class.' I chose to be positive with that person and shared my positive point of view about my yoga experience, which won over the negative experience my brain experienced.

I don't want to make it sound like I want to share just the positivity. I encourage people to try something new, tell them the bright side of it and let them create their own positive or negative experience. With my positive opinions, I'm sure they will experience new things, explore new places, try some exotic food or watch a movie. If I'd shared a negative experience, they would have bad expectations and maybe they would never try it, just because I made them hate it already. It's another example showing that you CAN change the world!

CHAPTER THIRTY-NINE

PEOPLE AND THEIR MISSION

Sometimes I wonder if people still love what they do and love their dreams after twenty or forty years of their occupation. Sometimes I really care about them. I think about my teachers, if they still love teaching the same things, if they feel they are important with a mission. I hope so. I hope they love what they do, even though I can't imagine myself in that position, which is a good thing, because the world needs every occupation. Every cleaner, postman, forest worker, officer or politician is very important and irreplaceable.

We all have dreams, hopes and missions. With a career, we start with something after school and, if we really like it, we stick with it, develop our talent, get promoted and constantly work on ourselves. Or we stop liking what started a year ago and, from being a salesperson, we move to a gardener because we want to pursue our passion for nature and we find ourselves there. Or, in some cases, we have no idea what we want to do for years and years, we learn about us and explore our gifts and sometimes test our patience.

Whether you know what you want or not, always take the first step, take the opportunity that is waiting for you, make sure you enjoy what you do and see purpose in it. If you're not happy, leave the job or the thing you've started and move on from any situation you might be in or any circumstances. Try to work out what is the best next step for you!

You might be doing the same things after thirty years, but if you know why you do it, you'll want to wake up every day and have the feeling that the world needs you and you're here to help, educate, open someone's eyes, make people happier or just be someone's assistant. We are here for ourselves, to enjoy our time, and we should love it. Also, we are here for our brothers and sisters who need our help. Now find the balance.

CHAPTER FORTY

COMPLIMENTS

My definition of a compliment is: 'A kind gesture of admiration received or given by someone.' I've been surrounded by compliments all my life, either giving or receiving. I think any form of compliment is beautiful.

Let's start with getting compliments. People are funny with receiving compliments. Instead of the pleasure of feeling great, they feel awkward and they don't know how to respond, or they feel obliged to give a compliment back so as not to be rude. If someone gives a compliment and you don't know why or you don't agree, always accept it. Those people wanted to give you a compliment, so just say 'thank you' and carry on.

When you compliment someone's clothes or smile or their house, you do it either because you want to make them happy or you do it because you mean it and it is simply your opinion. Either way, people are thankful for your compliment and, trust me, they will never get sick of your compliments. We all love them. They make us feel good, right?

If someone is down and you want to make their day brighter, give them a compliment. It is a beautiful way to spread positive energy and love around us because, when we compliment people and mean it, we plant a seed of love in them. They'll feel loved, beautiful and they'll definitely be carrying the seed of love for the rest of their lives.

CHAPTER FORTY-ONE

ADMIRE

The world is an incredible place to live. We have crystal-clear oceans, beautiful countryside, colourful animals, modern cities, smart inventions etc. It's incredible what nature can create and what a human brain can invent. We are constantly moving forward, getting new ideas, exploring new places and trying to make the world better and our lives easier. If you just stop for a moment and look around, you can see all the amazing natural treasures and all the ideas created by a very smart person.

When I see something truly amazing I always say to myself: 'Wow this is a miracle, what a gift the person had, and what a gift we have to experience it all!' I think about the beginning of the process; how it was made, who came up with the idea, how many years it took them to find the solution, to find the last ingredient, how many failures the person must've gone through. I'm astonished by inventions such as computers, electricity, glass in windows, drugs, contact lenses, the internet, complicated surgeries... all the things that must have taken ages to come up with.

Admiring is a beautiful part of our lives. It makes us smile (sometimes even with our mouth open) and our eyes sparkle. Admiring makes us even more curious, and the fact you've explored something new or admired a plant you haven't seen before leaves you astonished, grateful and thinking what a miracle it is that we get to live and how many incredible and unexplained inventions, animals and all other admirable things surround us. We become hungry, wanting to see more, explore more and admire more.

If we admire, we are amazed and impressed. We have the happy state in our mind that something similar or new we haven't discovered will appear very soon, because there are still so many things to explore. That's why it's essential to try new things all the time; try new food, explore five blocks behind your house, travel to a completely different country, use new brands of washing powder because, by doing things like this, we can admire new, beautiful details we haven't noticed before, or we can get a whole new idea about how things work. By doing this, we become more open-minded and we'll never get bored.

CHAPTER FORTY-TWO

RESOLUTIONS

Sometimes I wonder if it's worth it to chase my dreams, follow my ideas, keep my progress going and be strict with my resolutions. Some deep voice inside of me is telling me: 'Of course, yeah, don't give up!' It's usually the tough voice from motivational videos I see online. I don't want to say I am about to give up on my dreams; I am ambitious and I really want to finish what I've started but, sometimes, I need to be sensible and know that even though I've started something, promising myself I'll finish, I really don't have to if I change my mind. Let's say it's reading a book I promised myself to finish. If I don't find the book interesting after twenty pages, I can stop and move on to another book. It's a promise I gave only to myself, no one else! Just me and my brain. Suddenly I can hear two voices; one of them is the proud voice saying: 'You have to finish the book because you made yourself a promise!' The other voice is saying: 'Why should you finish the book and waste your time if you do not like it, just because you promised?'

So what should I do now? 'Hey mind, can you please leave me alone?'

Whenever I decide to end something before I'm finished, I give myself three good reasons why I should. I move on and keep my mind clear by getting rid of the things I promised, things I don't need any more or I've stopped being excited about. When you are working on something and you don't see the meaning of it, you're just doing it because you gave yourself this stupid resolution or you promised it to someone else. Then, on the other side, you work on something you love. You're passionate about your goal and it doesn't have to make any sense to anyone else because you're determined and certain your hard work makes sense and you see the meaning in what you're doing. Once you've finished, you're so happy, with a grateful heart that you didn't give up and the feeling that you can tick off another resolution because you were following your purpose.

That's the final destination of our resolutions. We make resolutions for some result we seek and, once we have achieved that, we get the satisfaction and move on.

CHAPTER FORTY-THREE

JUDGING

We all judge as humans. It is natural. We all have certain beliefs, opinions, standards, and if someone is doing otherwise, we naturally don't like it, and it doesn't feel good and we judge it. But we can learn how to control our judgement. Why? Because judging others too much breaks a trust with other people; if they see how much we judge others, they won't come to us to confide, they won't tell us their biggest secrets because they'll be scared of us judging them.

It is important to develop a trustful relationship with people around you, not only when you keep a promise you won't reveal a secret to anyone, but also when you respect the opinions of others and support their dreams. If someone is brave enough to share their life stories with you, if they come to see you seeking advice about a thing they're ashamed of, or they have something unacceptable to society on their heart that everyone else would normally judge, your reaction is very important. We, as always, can choose how we react to things and how we react to people. When a friend comes out to you that they're gay, or they owe thousands to the bank, or tell you they have a disease that people usually judge, or they mention they haven't watched that famous classic movie, or they are ashamed or scared of something that no one else is, just give them a hug for the courage they've shown. You can usually see how important their confession is to them. Try to understand them, be cool with them. If they want to, try to talk about it with them and, crucially, never laugh, refuse or make disgusted faces.

We all judge in our brains, but to improve the mental health of people we care about, we need to be very careful and try to focus on how much we judge in front of others. One day it might be you who'll have a problem or be in a trouble, and all you'll want will be a friend you can say anything you need to, knowing you'll be heard and not judged.

CHAPTER FORTY-FOUR

BE EXCITED

Being excited about life in general is one of the best approaches you can have. Being enthusiastic is a quality people around you love, and is the extra that makes your personality extraordinary. It is the magnet that attracts new and exciting things into your life because, by having the sparkle in you, you attract like-minded people and you'll become surrounded by people who are excited about things too. They are excited about their work, families and hobbies. You can really see their passion, and when you are surrounded by people like this and you see their excitement, it really inspires you and gives you the answer to why you are here, why you do what you love.

I've met many people who were excited about their lives. I could genuinely feel their passion and excitement, whether they were producers, artists, receptionists, police officers. Their sparkle was real and I knew I could trust them. When people are excited about what they do, it means they know why they do it and see the meaning. I can always trust these people and their intentions. So, whenever you have the energy and opportunity to be enthusiastic, do it!

CHAPTER FORTY-FIVE

SHINE

If you get an invitation, show up! If you have an opportunity, grab it! If you are going to meet some new people, be you and be your best! Always think that this is the chance to present yourself and show everyone who you are. If I go somewhere really important, I go there with one mission: 'They must remember me!' I want to shine so bright people will never forget me. I want to connect and network with other people who are passionate about happiness, love, art, equality, performing and make-up, talking about who we are and why we are here.

Especially in our twenties, we want to reach our dreams quickly. We want to build a company, establish a brand, start a business and, in most cases, we need to be our best to impress those we might be working with because our future clients or co-workers need someone to look up to, be inspired by. They need to see the passion and the energy of you in general.

I want to show who I am and what I can do to as many people as possible, so I smile and I'm enthusiastic and I feel

I'm always the big bubble there. That's me. That's why I shine. I shine because I promote myself and I get satisfaction from making other people happier and inspiring everyone. That's why I shine; I have the passion for life.

We all shine. For different reasons, in different environments, we all shine. You can shine at any time; when you want to let the world you are there, when you go to a family party, when you walk down the street. You can shine when you are by yourself in the park if you're not a people person. Always remember, you shine, and your unique beams of light can reach other people's hearts.

CHAPTER FORTY-SIX

IF YOU DON'T CHANGE, THEY WILL CHANGE

You know who you are and you love being yourself. Then you find a new job or join a new club and there are people who behave differently to you, with different values and beliefs. They might be more negative, too. In the beginning you are doing great; you keep it strong, follow your beliefs and keep your amazing attitude. But then it comes. Because you are the only one who behaves differently, it's very easy to be dragged down by the negativity and the majority of the people around you. I'm writing about this because I've experienced that.

After living in Sydney my energy levels were so high and I was smiling, was very optimistic and extremely happy, and everyone who saw me or crossed paths with me was leaving happier after meeting me. I could see that, but suddenly I started to complain more in London. I started to talk negatively about people, even started using phrases like my workmates when I didn't want to. I knew it wasn't nice and

I knew that wasn't me. So I went back to my roots. I spent more time by myself and I became stronger. I stayed positive and happy no matter how they seemed to be putting me down.

And then, after persisting with their negativity, something amazing happened. People changed. People started talking to me differently, acting differently. Just around me, though. With the rest of the crew or workmates they stayed the same. They noticed my inner power, my strength, kindness, love, happiness and they started liking it. They started mentioning things I never thought they would even know. They tried to have a conversation about mindfulness, yoga and energy, and they complained less around me and talked nicely about other people. Basically, there was less and less bullshit. They still had the same mean, hurtful, negative chat with other workmates but, as long as they approached me, they always gave me a smile or said something nice. It was crazy, like a miracle. I had to laugh. I could feel that wasn't in their nature and knew it was fake. I really enjoyed this 'fake' behaviour because it made me realise that, by just being me and standing up for my values and keeping my positive energy, I change the environment around me in a good way, in the way I like it. Without forcing it.

My intention is never to try to change anyone, but I'm always so flattered when someone comes to me and tells me: 'You taught me how to be a happier person. You showed me how to complain less. I've learnt how to love myself.'

It's beautiful to stay who you are. Sometimes it's challenging, but you can stay strong, just to impact other people's lives with your good intentions. One thing I know for sure: if you have good intentions, you feel so pure, you feel strong, because no one can hurt you.

CHAPTER FORTY-SEVEN

TIME

You have the choice to decide how to spend your life, therefore you are responsible for every moment of your life. One day, when I was cleaning the shelves at the bar where I worked, I realised I was responsible for the next few minutes of that moment. I realised I had the choice to choose my mood, my conversation, my attitude! I decided to choose fun for the rest of my life. While I was cleaning the bar, I realised I could be miserable and complain to my colleague or I could be happy and joke about everything. The time will pass anyway and tomorrow you'll look back at today thinking about your decisions. Whenever I realise the power of the moment and that I'm the one in charge of the quality of my time, I always think about the future and how I feel after making my decision. For example, if I have a big day or an important event on the next day, I know I shouldn't drink much alcohol the previous night. When I'm in front of the decision of whether to drink or not, I always think about the next day, about how I will feel, how my body will feel. I have a conversation with myself and am self-aware about all the decisions I'm making.

It is the same with any mood you're experiencing right now. If you are aware of how you're feeling and you don't like where you are at this moment or how you feel, you have the power to change it right now. If you know how to fix the problem today, if you know the decision is up to you and you know something will change after your decision, you can create a better future for yourself right now.

We all have the same amount of time. Sometimes we figure out things later than others, but that's OK, because even though we do have the same amount of time, we all have different timings for figuring things out, making mistakes, learning about ourselves and who we are etc.

Also, with our timing, it's very important to be patient with ourselves while we are going where we want to be, while we're figuring out who we are and working on our dreams. For me, in my twenties, even though I'm really impatient and want to achieve my dream right now and want to have everything today, I know very well how important it is to be patient and gentle with myself. I know I have my own timing, my journey planned and all I need to do is relax, calm the fuck down and just enjoy the process. I need to enjoy every day of my life, breathe, be present, don't rush things, don't compare myself with other people who are the same age as me and 'made it further' in life or make more money than me. I need to remind myself it is their destiny and their own life and I have my own plan; everything that is happening to me has its perfect timing. All I need to do is to work on myself, my work plan, my own goals. If there is anything I can work on, I do it, and do it 100 per cent. When I've done everything I could possibly do, I just relax and trust the process.

Patience is so important while you go where you want to be. You have your plan, so stick to it. You have your strategy, so follow it. You have the faith, so get closer and closer each day. Do not underestimate the power of your daily routine. Even when you can't see any progress day to day, you do grow and you do get closer to your dream; every breath counts, every drop of sweat, every word, every mile, every phone call, every 'failure', every minute. When all the work is done and you got into the body shape you wanted, wrote a book, won the competition, achieved your big goal, you will look at it as one whole creation, and you'll forget those little painful moments, sighs, cries, feelings of giving up, frustration, anger. You'll be proud of your masterpiece, whatever it is.

Imagine your dream, work, goal is a field full of hundreds of flowers. The field is very special. The field has only one flower of each species and every day you can plant only one seed. The diversity of the field is then up to you; if you plant a new flower every day, or if you skip a few days and therefore miss a few colours that could be in your field. You can stop after one week and have seven different flowers, or you can stop after a year and have 365 flowers. It is the same with you and your journey; you plant a seed every day and you wait patiently until you have the field of flowers that makes you happy.

CHAPTER FORTY-EIGHT

THE TIME IS NOW! THE TIME IS RIGHT

'When I have this and that I swear I'll be happier and I will finally feel better.' We hear this around all the time. Sometimes we say it too, not knowing the time we have is now and that we are the creators of our lives, at this moment! Yes, this moment! Right now we can decide what to do, how we want to feel, how to spend the rest of our lives! We can wake up every morning and decide that we'll be happy for the whole day. We can start a discipline, new habits, tick something off the bucket list and say how we feel right now.

I have so many new ideas all the time and I'm pretty sure you do, too. The question is: how many of our ideas do actually happen? And how many of our ideas will never leave our brain and won't see the light? I'll be honest; I tend to put things off. I think everyone does it sometimes. I always think there will be time to make new things, that there will be a day when I can explore the mountains I wanted to visit, and time to learn the new vocabulary I want to learn. For example, with this book, I have so many new ideas to share for new chapters, and I have so much to tell, and instead of writing it down I tell myself: 'You have time, you'll do it tonight or you'll get an even better idea later.' And guess what! I never do. Either I forget the idea or I get distracted by something else I prioritise in that moment, and then I start to wonder what I wanted to write about yesterday, what I wanted to share with the world or what I wanted to explain more deeply. The more it happens to me, the more often I write things down at the time I'm thinking about them, so I know it's out. If I don't have much time to write about it in detail, I'll get back to it later, but the fact it's written down is so freeing for me; I know I don't have to think about it any more, so my brain is 'clean and fresh' and ready for new ideas.

We can't wait in pain, uncertainty or fear for 'better times' because, right now, we are living the best times. Yes, we are! By the 'best times' I don't mean being on top of our career, celebrating earning money, drinking champagne and enjoying our fame and success. By 'best times' I mean the beauty of the present moment, the sweetness of presence, a celebration of being alive with everything that comes with it. Be grateful for the gift called life. All our emotions and feelings (e.g. struggles, frustrations and anger) are just labels, made up words that just help us to express how we feel. Obviously, diagnosed depression and similar illnesses are a different matter.

At any time, however, we might feel we have two choices:

1) We can change our reality if we don't like it.

If there is any emotion, usually negative, we wish to change, we can stop and ask ourselves: 'What is the next step I'm going to take to get where I want to be? How can I feel better? What decision do I need to make?' By asking these questions, we can move forward to the next level, to set ourselves free and therefore stop being victims of our own time, our own lives.

2) We can't change our reality.

We can find ourselves in a situation when we feel hopeless because there is nothing we can do to change it. We feel heartbroken, worried, unmotivated, lost, and we don't know why. In those moments, you know what I do? I sit down, close my eyes, connect with myself and say: 'Be with it, be where you are and enjoy it.' Even though it hurts so much, even though it's not pleasant, sit with your feelings, accept where you are all the way, believing that these times are in your life to show you something new, beautiful, exciting, to lead you to a new and exciting path, to make you stronger, to teach you new things about life and maybe teach you something new about yourself. If we really can't change our reality right now, let's be with it there, fully present.

No matter how difficult it is for you right now, you be there, OK? Be all there. 'Enjoy' the discomfort, pain, break-up, struggle, betrayal, journey, refusal, financial struggles. Accept it and take it as a part of you growing. You become stronger, more patient, irresistible. Trust the process and the journey, believe it's happening to you for some reason and, even though it doesn't feel good right now, you're going further, in the right direction. I love you. I believe in you. I am with you.

I love the quote by Bertrand Russell: 'Time we enjoy wasting is not wasted time.' Whenever I feel lazy, unmotivated, weak, thinking I should get one page of my book done but just can't force myself to do anything, even make food, I just smile. I stop being hard on myself and enjoy my mood, body, emotions and I watch a movie or do something fun because resting, doing nothing and feeling distracted is an important part of our development too.

If you really want to do something now but the voices (society, childhood, friends) tell you no, don't listen to them. We live our own lives, we have a unique body metabolism, unique DNA, unique abilities and skills and we have our unique clock. Going to bed at 10pm can be early for me and can be late for you. We shouldn't worry what others do at certain times or we shouldn't feel bad if we are the only ones in the classroom who don't like getting up early. If you really feel like wiping the dust on your shelves at midnight, do it. Don't wait for Saturday morning because one day your mum told you that cleaning day is only on Saturday. Eat your breakfast three hours after waking up because you feel like it, even though all nutritionists tell you it's not good for your body. Go for a fabulous brunch on a Monday morning despite the fact 'you are supposed to hate Mondays and be at work, and brunch on Sundays'. Basically, do whatever you feel at the time; listen to your body clock, your inner voice and feel your own rhythm.

CHAPTER FORTY-NINE

YOU ARE NOT MISSING OUT

I used to worry about missing out on great parties when I couldn't go or the beautiful sunsets when I was at work, I was always thinking I wasn't in the right place at the right time. I was thinking that people might have more fun than me while I can't because I'm stuck somewhere else on some 'less fun' event. With social media, we can see what our friends are doing right now or what they did last in the last twenty-four hours. We see them having fun everywhere and sometimes we might feel we missed out. We weren't there when they had 'the best time' of their lives and we wish we had been.

The thing is, we need to take responsibility for our own lives and know what we expect from today, what we want to do and how we want to feel. If you decided to go to bed at 9pm last night reading your book, having a bath or meditating, you made this decision because you wanted to; it was your choice. The next day when you see your friend's story from last night, you might feel you missed out because they had more fun than you. Just because they were drinking and dancing doesn't mean you had less fun. You had your own kind of fun. You chose to do what you love to do, you wanted that, so believe that anything you decide to do is happening at the perfect timing and all you have to do is to enjoy what you have.

Also, don't forget a balance is very important too – we party and we relax. One day I was having a lazy day and thinking: 'You should go out and have fun,' even though I had an amazing night the night before. I didn't realise that recovery, relaxation, just chilling in general is an important part of having fun too because I can't party all the time. I need to take it easy to have more amazing times in the future and, while I'm taking it easy, I shouldn't punish myself for missing out on events others are experiencing that moment.

The secret to being happy where you are is to make the most of every situation. It can be waiting or going through something unpleasant or it can be the missed train to the festival and all you can do is to say: 'Right, what am I going to do with myself now, how will I use the time I have?' You can take advantage of those two hours you 'missed' and you can start doing something completely random and new you wouldn't have done otherwise. You can start writing or you can meet some interesting people and learn new things. It is all in your head and how you look at things. If you believe everything that happens to you happens at the right time, providing you with the best experience, you'll fall in love with every moment of your life and you'll live meaningfully and enjoyably.

CHAPTER FIFTY

EVERYTHING THAT HAPPENS IS RIGHT

You can create a happiness moment right now by being happy with everything that is happening around you or to you. The peace is gone when you start thinking about what you think should be happening right now, or what you would like to be happening right now. If you are fully aware of where you are and accept that, you're at peace with yourself, with your life.

You can choose if you want to plan your holiday properly day by day or if anything you'll do will be spontaneous. In both cases, you always make the right choice. Anything that's happened to me was simply perfect. It happened in the right place at the right time and, when I look back, it all makes sense.

For example, one summer I went to a festival and saw a few shows. Every show left something deep inside me and I got a particular idea from each, so everything inspired me. Every comedian told jokes and had a sense of humour or ideas I wouldn't have experienced if I hadn't gone there. At another show I would get a different idea that would create a whole new story to tell. So I just want to tell you to relax and trust; don't be stressed about events you think you might miss, don't regret you didn't go to this 'important' party or a meeting you were supposed to go to. The decisions you make or the circumstances that are following you at the time are right. Everything that happens in our lives is just right; it is our experience and our destiny.

CHAPTER FIFTY-ONE

LIVE SO FULLY YOU WILL HAVE NO REGRETS

When I was working at a coffee shop serving an older man and I was enthusiastic and bubbly, happy to be alive, I was wondering if he was looking at me thinking: 'I wish I was happy like her when I was her age.'

The older I am, the more often I realise the power of the present moment, the gift, the responsibility. I know I'm responsible for my present moment, my future, so I live the fullest whenever I realise my existence.

Sometimes I see how miserable a situation can be or how sad everyone around me seems. In these cases, I realise I have the power to change it, so I tell a joke, or just dance or run around like crazy, just to create a better atmosphere. I love laughter and happy faces around me, so I know I need to become one in order to attract/create a happy atmosphere.

It is important to realise it as long as we are young. It is important to grab the chance, actually the responsibility, for the moment, for our own life. Whenever I'm procrastinating (doing things other than the ones I told myself I would do, just because I'm lazy), I often find myself in charge of my life. I find myself thinking: 'Hey you! Now! This is the time! You should be doing this. You said you would do this, so why are you just scrolling down social media and not writing the book you wanted to write so much?' In that moment, I realise my existence and I have only two choices. Either keep procrastinating or give myself 'a slap' and start doing something more important or useful.

The fuller we live, the deeper we feel, the longer moments we cherish.

Enjoying little things:

It's so important to enjoy every moment of your life and be present at every moment because, one day (and it happens), you'll look back and start wondering about those few last years. You'll start wondering whether you have some nice memories or whether you've lived to the fullest so far. And if you live every day to the fullest, take risks, feel the rain on your skin, be spontaneous, smile at strangers, you'll be satisfied with the life you live. You'll have no regrets about living differently, there won't be a moment you'd like to change or anything you wish you'd done better.

In my case, it's travelling. I know the time is not going to stop and if I can I travel now, why not? Let's have some adventures now. It can be cheap, can be for two nights only but, by travelling while young, I give myself the memories, ticking off the boxes and making my life meaningful, exciting and memorable. By travelling I prove to myself I'm doing great, and I live life to the fullest. The life I want. If you live every moment to the fullest, it'll be easy to go back there any time.

CHAPTER FIFTY-TWO

TRAVELLING

I believe travelling is essential in our lives. It is as important as reading or any other form of education because, by travelling, we learn. As we constantly learn through our lives, we become wiser, and travelling is one of the fastest ways to learn, explore and see all the beauty around us. We not only learn about other countries and their cultures, but we learn about ourselves. We learn how far we can go with our limits, dedication and patience.

In Australia I learnt it is possible to live a stress-free life. In Beijing I found out I don't need to speak Chinese to smile or to show how many pieces of fruit I want. In Italy I learnt how to be passionate about everything. Denmark introduced me to hygge (a quality of cosiness and comfortable conviviality that engenders a feeling of contentment or well-being) and London made me the most open-minded person.

Travel as much as you can. If you are on a budget, book hostels and use buses. If someone wants to take you out, go with them. Having a day off and it's sunny? Day trip! That forest next to your town, the one which you've been wondering how it looks? Go and explore! Sometimes you don't need to take planes to see natural treasures or breathtaking wonders; sometimes it can be right in front of you.

When I travel, I'm not only relaxing and recharging, I'm observing. I observe what lives people live and how different the landscape can be, comparing it with my country and what energy that certain place gives me. I observe how people talk to each other and what gestures they use, the pace of the place and, from all of that, I learn. I observe, learn and use all the information further in my life, share the knowledge with my friends, in my work and, when I get inspired somewhere, I use the local ideas or design in decorating my own home, so the holiday memory lives on. If someone's kindness and love really impress me, I remember that and try to work on myself to be a better human.

The more places I visit, the more open-minded I become and the less judgemental I am, because different cultures show me it is not me who has the right lifestyle, the right way of living and the right social norms and manners. I simply realise everyone in the world lives their lives in their happy way. They are happy with their food, tradition, religion, way of communication. I have no right to judge anything thinking my life is better or more valuable. We all can find our happiness everywhere, regardless of where we are from.

CHAPTER FIFTY-THREE

EMBRACE YOUR UNIQUENESS

There is always an ideal example in something; in life, in a partner, in behaviour, beauty, society. It is a perfection which means one thing: expectations. You're not supposed to meet the expectations in your life, but to embrace your persona, character, behaviour, body and all of your gifts that might seem 'weird' to most people just because they don't know about it. They have closed minds or are too judgemental. Anyway, no one should make you feel less beautiful, less special or less confident. For example, you like a certain fetish in your sex life and, just because most of your friends find it disgusting or weird, it doesn't mean there is something wrong with you. Or you like to bleach your eyebrows, smell your partner's armpits, to sit while peeing when you're a man, like to eat your nails or wear clothes society doesn't approve of because they don't meet the gender norms. Whatever you do and however you want to express yourself, if it makes you happy and you don't hurt anyone, do it as often as you desire. Enjoy it, embrace it!

Even if you don't want to stand out or you don't want to be rebellious, you still need to accept your unique gifts, talents, behaviours and, as they call it, your weirdness. If there is anything you have but others don't, don't try to fit in or please others; be proud of what you have. Remember Oscar Wilde's quote: 'Be yourself; everyone else is already taken.'

CHAPTER FIFTY-FOUR

AIM HIGH

I'm always hungry, always go for more, want to try more, see more, explore more. I'm happy where I am while going for better and better at all times. This is a hard one because, sometimes, this feeling of wanting more or moving faster and faster towards goals can be very dangerous, because it can make us feel greedy. We should always appreciate and be grateful for what we have, be humble and realise how blessed we are to have our basic human needs met (back to the gratitude). This is so important to remember. There is nothing wrong with having the best car or luxurious holidays or designer clothes, but once you get to the point where you want more and more because you're not happy or you think you never have enough, then you should slow down, get back to your values and maybe think of the reasons why you want the things you don't have and why the things would make you happier.

If there is anything you want to become better at and you know how, do it.

Knowing you've tried everything you can to get where you want to is enough.

Here are some tips to help you to get closer to your biggest dreams and, therefore, a happy life. It's basically all about being open and saying yes:

Go for interviews

If there is a job position you always wanted and you see there is a vacancy, definitely apply, and do everything you can to get it. Send emails, introduce yourself and show the best of you and everything you can do. Aim high, hope for the best and, if they send you an email with a 'No' or if they don't send you a reply at all, just get over it. Don't ask yourself what is wrong with you and why you didn't succeed. What if they remember you and contact you in a year and, in the meantime, you'll get exactly the right experience from another job you needed but didn't have before? Now you can shine! Always be proud that at least you tried because, as they say: 'You never regret the things you did. You regret the things you didn't.'

Enter competitions

As a kid and a teenager, I entered so many competitions. I want to share with you and give you some reasons why you should enter competitions in your field. I just put myself out there. I knew I loved to shine and I loved the attention, so I was hosting fashion shows at my high school, three years in a row. I was representing our school in singing, dancing and art competitions. I even tried *The Idol*.

When I moved to London, I didn't know anyone and all I wanted to do was be seen, get into a circle of like-minded people, be creative and dance, so I entered every beauty competition, dance competition, transgender beauty competition, just to show who I was. Sometimes I was realistic and knew there was only a small chance of winning, but I did it anyway. Sometimes I got surprised and ended up second. Sometimes I got eliminated in the first round when I believed in myself so much and wanted to get further.

I remember the first transgender competition I entered. There were performers doing a number during the break and we shared the backstage. They loved the way I was doing my make-up and saw something in me. One year later, I was touring UK festivals with them. It is all about doing your best at the time.

Network

Think of what field you want to be the best, then make some business cards and go out! Whenever you see a potential client or future work, go and introduce yourself, have a chat and leave them your business card. It's the first seconds when you can impress and leave something special and unforgettable about you in that person.

Because I need to make money myself and I don't depend on anyone, I am a hustler and a go-getter. I try to connect with as many people in my field as possible, other make-up artists, LGBT people, performers, trying to get a bit further step by step, closer to my dream day by day. I just message everyone I consider a possible work opportunity, who could help me or I can help them, who could introduce me to this guy who organises that big party or anyone who knows the editor of the magazine. I just want to get everywhere. If they don't answer, fine. I tried. If they answer but are not interested, fine. I tried. I contact everyone where I can see a possible chance or potential. I am not gonna lie; sometimes I contact them with a little bit of fear, especially if that email or gig seems really important, but at the end I am so happy I did it. Regardless of the outcome of the correspondence or conversations, I know I tried, so I have no question marks in my head asking: 'What if?'

When I don't succeed, I don't take it as a failure, don't beat myself with regrets for trying and wasting my time rehearsing, getting ideas and practising. I tap myself on the shoulder because the whole experience gave me new ideas and opportunities. I improved or learnt something new. I stay focused and ready for some next adventure.

I don't even feel ashamed, because I don't care who laughed at me or criticised me. I know I did my best; I am proud of myself because I put myself out there, tried what I wanted to try and I did it all for myself, for no one else (even your proud parents won't give you more satisfaction than your proud self).

CHAPTER FIFTY-FIVE

NEVER FAILURES, ALWAYS LESSONS

I want to share one last thing about growing and going higher. Making mistakes.

Do not be afraid to make mistakes! (By the way, don't you think it should be called 'a try that didn't work out'? It sounds so much nicer, without shame or guilt, right?)

Your life is not a competition or an exam where you need to show only the best of yourself, when the flaws are judged or criticised. Don't be afraid to be vulnerable, fragile, sensitive, to try new things even when you think it won't work out. You will be so happy you tried your best and now you know how it feels to experience what you wanted to try regardless of the outcome. You can tick it off and move on. You know you did it. You can be satisfied even though things didn't work out according to the plan.

Whenever you make a decision that didn't seem to be right that moment but you did it anyway, or you disappointed someone or you 'didn't pay your parking ticket and got a fine, or you simply said something that wasn't true and now it got you into trouble, please, please, please do not regret anything. Do not wish to take it back or change it. You did it, found out it wasn't right, learnt; you will do better next time and you can move on. Mistakes are here in our lives to tell us that we can be better tomorrow, that we still can show how amazing we are, how loyal we can be, how irresistible in some situations. We should be grateful for the mistakes we make because they lead us to the right direction, to the brighter future, setting us free and taking us where we are meant to be.

The courage of trying is so rewarding, and much stronger than the possible chance of experiencing a failure.

CHAPTER FIFTY-SIX

DON'T TAKE ANYTHING TO HEART

I f someone gives you a compliment it warms your heart, makes you happy, because you allow it. If someone gives you negative feedback, it makes you angry, sad, because you allow it.

Imagine we are all in bubbles. I'm in my own bubble and you are in yours, and we are all talking, singing, screaming our opinions, but no one can hear us. We just talk for ourselves. Now imagine that you can invite other people to your bubble and share your thoughts, opinions and ideas with them. They hear you out and, if they like what you say, they stay in your bubble and, because they like you, you want to stay in their bubble. If they don't like what you say, they leave your bubble, and if you don't like what they say, you can leave their bubble too.

It is so similar in our real lives. You can tell me whatever you think about me, qualities I have and qualities I miss, how I am and how I should be according to you. You can give me the sweetest compliment. You can tell me that my eyes are so beautiful but, if I don't think so, I won't believe you, so

I won't take it personally. If you tell me my singing is horrible, I can listen to you if I enter your bubble but, because I love my voice and I love the way I sing, I will leave your bubble and I won't listen to you. I won't take anything you said personally. You see, there is no difference between positive or negative feedback. The difference is how you respond.

Another example of how to follow your beliefs and your inner voice: imagine you are in a room full of colour-blind people but you don't know about it. Your whole life you see yourself as brunette. You love your hair colour so much but, surprisingly, the rest of the class see your hair as blonde and they love it so much too. You are confused because, all your life, you thought you were brunette, but now everyone tells you you're blonde, so you start believing it. Because you like the fact everyone loves your blonde hair and gives you compliments, and even though you never wanted to be blonde, you start to love your 'new blonde' hair, even though you liked your brunette hair before as well. You start to think you really are blonde and start to love yourself even more. After some time, you leave the room, so happy about your blonde hair, so excited to show everyone in the world how beautiful your colour is, but everyone starts laughing at you because they see your colour as ginger and they hate it. You are confused again because you thought you were blonde. So you don't know where the truth is and what to think. The truth is, you shouldn't listen to any of the people. Neither those who gave you compliments about your hair colour, nor those who were laughing at you and didn't like it. You should've believed in your colour in the room with colour-blind people and, whatever anyone else said, you wouldn't have cared, because you knew your truth.

So it's the same with everyone in your real life. Whatever they tell you, it is none of your business. You know who you are, what you do and where you are going. As long as you know your truth, don't let anyone tell you who you are, what you do and where you should go. Don't let anyone go to your bubble.

CHAPTER FIFTY-SEVEN

I DON'T ENVY

I used to envy other people when I was younger. I envied because I wanted to have what they had or to be where they were. I was envious when other make-up artists got goodies for free from make-up brands, when other performers got their gig, when people were on holidays when I was working or at school. I didn't know that everything comes in the right time and in a perfect order. In the last few years, by reading a lot of self-help books, spiritual reads for self-awareness and mindfulness, I've learnt how to stop wanting what others have, to stop being envious and how to start being happy with what I already have, knowing everything has its timing.

It's actually very simple. I have two pieces of advice for you:

- Fall in love with everything you have and appreciate where you are.
- Focus on yourself and don't compare.

I was talking about appreciating and being grateful earlier in my book. If you are grateful, you are happy instantly.

So, if you stop right now and realise how much you are blessed already, you'll become satisfied with the way you live. Just think about how much you've done already in your life, the places you've visited, people you've met. Count your qualities: how loyal you are, how much fun, how understanding you can be. Think about all the talents you have, how many things you wanted that you already have. It doesn't have to be only material things in your life you should be grateful for. Of course you can get the most expensive cars and clothes and buy them because they make you happy and you enjoy wearing or using them. There is nothing wrong with spending lots of money if you can afford it and if you love it, but remember, buying stuff shouldn't become a competition with others; you shouldn't prove to others what you can buy and that you follow the latest trend. Simply, anything you spend money on, do it for yourself. It should please you, not them.

If you focus on yourself and your life path, you'll become happier because you won't compare your life with others. You'll know your path is unique, that you live in a particular place, have this type of body that is beautiful the way it is, that your behaviour is special and people love it. You'll fall in love with everything you have. You may have noticed that tour guide horses in cities wear blinkers over their eyes to not get distracted by other vehicles, people or any fast movement. They follow their path peacefully as that's the only thing they can see. This should be the same with us.

This example of horses should encourage us to stay focused on our journey, wherever we might be or however slow we think we go. Our mood shouldn't worsen because of the way other people live, and we shouldn't get frustrated by the achievements of our friends. We simply should be happy with what we have and where we are.

Don't get me wrong, being comfortable where you are is not the same as being happy where you are. If you are comfortable where you are, that's nice, but it can get boring eventually. Also, I think it's impossible to be comfortable and happy where you are forever. You'll realise you want to do different things as you get older and you'll start to get bored You'll have new ideas and new dreams and you'll want to achieve them. Being happy with what you have is a blessing because you know that, even though you're not comfortable where you are or you don't have the job you want right now, you know you are on the right path towards your destiny. You'll be wise because you'll know, no matter what others achieve, you are walking your unique path. You'll know that, wherever you are, there is something you're supposed to learn or explore or realise, that every chapter of your life has its own message, meaning and lesson. So, yeah, it is possible to be happy where you are with what you have, even though it's not where you want to be or what you want right now.

Whenever you feel people are achieving more than you, firstly focus on yourself and, secondly, remember one of my favourite quotes for being happy where you are: 'Don't compare your life to others. There is no comparison between the sun and the moon. They shine when it's their time.'

I used to compare my life when I was seventeen with Lady Gaga's. I was sad and sometimes even depressed because I wasn't famous yet. I wanted to sing and travel the world and have my fans, but I was living in my village of 1,000 people and was frustrated the world didn't know me. I've always had the desire to show who I am and to be seen and, at that time, I was so unhappy because the combination of my desire that wasn't fulfilled yet with comparing myself with Gaga was just killing me and making me depressed and uncomfortable where I was. I wanted to be in her shoes immediately. I wasn't enjoying my own path, my environment, friends, experiences; I was so impatient and wanted to skip this part of my life just to be twenty-seven (that was the time when I thought I'd be famous) and show the world my message and who I was.

When I think about it now, I laugh, but at that time I really felt down as I wanted to be big immediately. A few years later, I know that my life's been wonderful and I enjoy every day and everything that comes my way. I'm grateful when I can go to the park with my best friend, for interviews that didn't happen as I wanted because I got an even better job. I'm grateful for being without my phone for a week when it got stolen twice in one year, because that made me more patient, and I had adventures I wouldn't normally have had if I'd still had my phone. Basically, wherever I find myself,

I know I'm going in the right direction, even when I feel lost, as we all sometimes do. Remember, whenever you're feeling lost, it's because you'll soon find a flame in your heart and experience something beautiful and exciting very, very soon. It's been like this my whole life, and in the life of others, too. So, don't worry, and remember this quote: 'I don't know where I'm going but I'm on my way.'

CHAPTER FIFTY-EIGHT

MEDITATE

I know it sounds like so much work to concentrate while sitting with your legs crossed, holding your thumb and index fingers together, smiling and, ideally, sitting by a waterfall.

Meditation is something that took me a long time to work out. Everyone was talking about it, but I didn't really know what to do and how to start. I started with an app on my phone and I did it for weeks. This really taught me how to be mindful, to be present and how to be aware of my own thoughts. I see meditation as a connection with my inner self, as a way to maintain my inner peace, in my body and mind. Actually, it is the only peaceful place where we can go to if we experience any distraction around us.

Today, I would describe meditation as a state of mind, when I realise nothing but my own world and everything happening within, which is my breath and my thoughts, thoughts that just flow so I don't have to think about anything. When I meditate, I focus on my breathing and, if there is any thought, I let it go and imagine my brain is empty without any thoughts, and when I find myself having another thought, I do the same again.

I meditate/be mindful so many times a day. Most of the time it is a meditation on the go, just to remind myself I'm safe, peaceful and in my zone. I meditate when I'm walking from my house to the train station or anywhere basically. I find myself in the moment realising the presence and perceiving everything around me. I often ask myself: 'What is the colour of the building you're passing every day?' Basically, common things I pass every day, but I'm so overwhelmed by my own thoughts that I simply don't realise anything that's around me. By realising the present moment, I meditate while walking, because I don't think about anything else but the subjects around me that make me realise my being.

I love meditation on public transport, too, especially on the underground, because there is no internet, so I can't be on social media or listen to music because the carriage is sometimes very noisy. If I don't have a book to read, I look in front of me and beyond that point when it gets blurry, and in that moment I create a bubble between my world and the world around me, so I don't care what is going on around me. I focus on my breathing. I also do it with my eyes closed, which might be easier sometimes, especially when I'm feeling distracted. A public transport meditation is a great way to spend your time when you have a great opportunity to do 'nothing'. When we have 'nothing' to do, we are caught in our own thoughts, and we might think about our colleagues at work, or our holidays this summer. By letting our thoughts go (not only on public transport), we create 'a new room' in our consciousness that allows us to be more calm and peaceful.

Breathing

Breathing is the easiest way to connect with your mind and your body. Anywhere. Anytime. Once we find ourselves in a moment of worry, inner conflict, anger, hatred, rush or any disturbing state of mind that prevents us being in the present moment, we should start putting all our attention on our breathing. Make the present moment sacred, focus on your breath, as there is nothing more important in our world (Actually, is there?).

I've found out that a great opportunity to connect with myself and especially with my breath is the 'cat and cow' pose. This is one of the yoga poses that brings me into the state of relaxation immediately. You might find another pose working for you even more, but cat and cow is a great way to get in rhythm with your breathing because it makes you focus on your inhale and exhale. When you focus on your breathing and count to ten, you'll realise you were present the whole time focusing on nothing but your breath. That is the simplest way to connect with yourself.

Online

YouTube is an amazing way to meditate as well. You can literally choose what kind of meditation you like, how long, where and when. I usually do YouTube meditations before sleep and when I feel unmotivated. In that case, I do manifesting meditations. When I feel under pressure, I listen to nature noises and calming meditations. With every full moon I charge my crystals, lie down and play a full moon meditation. When I don't feel in harmony, I do chakra cleansing and activating meditations and, when I'm concerned about my income, I do a meditation for abundance and prosperity. Technology is offering meditation to a new generation. We can improve our mental health and our wellbeing in general by practising meditations through our phones and computers and get help from experts, yogis, monks, spiritual leaders and others who are accessible with a finger tap.

Body

When I feel overwhelmed, stressed, under pressure, confused, down or my mind is just wandering off, I 'organise myself'. Firstly, I start with a deep breath and tell myself to breathe deeply. I start with a deep inhale and count four inhales and five exhales, then I focus on my posture, on my shoulders to see if they're even, my facial muscles and whether they're relaxed, my chest to check if it's open, and my lower back, stomach and bottom to make sure they are in the right position. A body meditation is a quick way to 'fix' your brain and body immediately and carry on mindfully for the rest of the day.

Nature contact

Nature always calls us. Nature always wants me to leave my house and go out and connect. And I follow that voice and the desire. Whenever I'm there, I'm calm, I'm free, I'm present and connected to myself. I feel I am a part of nature, the smell makes me grounded and the sound of it relaxes me. I don't remember a time in nature when I wouldn't be present. When I look back at every single time of me being by the beach or in the forest or at the park, I remember exactly how I felt and what was going through my mind. Whenever you feel the urge to disconnect from people and connect to your own world, go out! Go for a run or a walk and just be by yourself. It is the best meditation you can do for yourself and it's free. I call it a free therapist, because I always feel like all the questions I had before my walk are answered after it. It works as a 'brain cleanse' whether you are in the mountains or a desert. You will feel lighter and the flow of your thoughts will become smoother, quieter and calmer.

CHAPTER FIFTY-NINE

SUCCESS

What is success? What does success mean to you? Is it a destination? Is it a state of mind?

To me, success is a rewarding feeling for your work, effort, energy. It is a feeling of accomplishment once you get where you wanted to be or even while you're still going to the destination, because success is the sweet feeling of fruition.

When I'm writing this book, I'm thinking that success is not defined by the number of copies of this book sold; success is the personal, intimate feeling between you and your accomplished goal. Success is the dream come true, the sweetness of your personal accomplishment and your own satisfaction, regardless of the outcome, the feedback and the external success. If you are happy with your work and proud of yourself looking back at the journey, that is success. Please, never compare your success with anyone else. Success is not comparable with anyone else. It is your baby, your journey and your work on yourself. Remember, once you start seeing yourself as a successful person, no one else's opinion will be important to you because you will know you are a creative master and a genius in your own world. So, now say to yourself: 'I am successful in anything I do.' Open up your wings and fly.

CHAPTER SIXTY

TREAT ME LIKE I AM GOING TO DIE TOMORROW

I had a thought the other day: why are some people nice to their friends and family members only before they know they are going to die soon? Why aren't they nice to them their whole life? Why are we nice to our close ones only on their birthday and at Christmas and not the whole year? I really wonder why. Why is being rude, offensive and violent (mentally or physically) in some cases more common than being nice, respectful and kind to each other?

I really want to live in a world where people:

Smile at each other

I understand we are all humans and we don't have to feel happy on the outside the whole time, but it really helps when we pass by our colleagues or even strangers in the streets and, without saying anything, just smile at them. Once you start smiling at people without a reason, once you trigger the positive avalanche, you will notice a significant difference in your daily life because people will give you their smile back in most cases and this will raise your endorphins and you will feel happy. I've been doing this for years and, even though I'm sometimes sad or upset about some things, going out and giving and receiving smiles always makes me feel loved and energetically uplifted.

When I'm at a cafe where the staff are not friendly, I try to give them my love and my smile, to make them feel good, as I never know what difficult customers they had to deal with before I came, or if their boss wasn't nice to them. When I smile they smile back, I express my gratitude and appreciation for their work, say 'thank you' and go to enjoy my coffee.

Also, when people see that you smile a lot and you're a happy person, they'll assume you're easy-going and friendly and can accept any task with ease, therefore you're more likely to get offers and new opportunities that frowning or grumpy people would probably not get. So, being a smiling person definitely helps you to get further in life, and attracts other smiling, happy people into your life. I know this all from my own experience, because wherever I go, I try to be the happiest person in the room, positive and enthusiastic. Sometimes I need to force it because of the circumstances, and sometimes I just don't smile at all, because there are days I just can't smile even when I want to. It's when I feel really down and I need to go to see people. We are all human beings and can't be smiling all the time but, please remember, when you realise you have the choice to smile and you don't suffer from deep sadness, depression or heavy anxiety, always choose a smile. Magical things will come to your life.

Help each other

By helping each other, I don't mean only helping the mum-of-two to carry the pram up the stairs, but helping our friends and co-workers with their daily struggles. If they feel down, cheer them up. If they are in financial need, lend them some money or buy them a lunch. If they are feeling stressed, ask them why and talk to them, give them your compassion, your help, your time, because that's the most valuable help you can ever get in life.

To me, helping someone is the sweetest feeling in the world, sweeter than any dessert I've tried. I just love giving a coin to a homeless person. I genuinely love it. Whenever I leave them any money I get warm goose bumps all over my body; I feel happier and my smile is shining so bright for a few minutes. I always tell myself: 'You're young but you're not poor, and this £1 won't kill you. One week from now you won't even remember and your wallet won't notice.' So I decided to give money at least once a day to anyone who needs it. What they need it for is not my business. The fact they need help in that moment is important.

Recently, I found out a friend from our neighbouring village back in Czechia is transgender as well, so I immediately reached out, as she was the first Czech trans person I knew.

We started chatting, she told me her story and I told her mine. Her dad doesn't accept her, her mum lives abroad, and because she's just nineteen years old and still studying, she needed to make money for her accommodation. I immediately took her under my wing; I genuinely felt like it was my responsibility to help her in her beginning and challenging times. Even though I couldn't help her financially, I wanted to be her best (trans) friend, someone she can talk to anytime. That day I'll never forget; I felt so happy and warm-hearted for the rest of my day. I was shining, confident and full of love.

I believe if we help each other every day, we can be high on life and we can fly. It can be anything! Anything! Do any of your family members need support in their personal life? Are any of your friends going through hard times at work or a break-up with their partner? Has your workmate been feeling down recently and you can tell they need to cheer up? Look around you; you can help everywhere, just open your heart, reach out and make the world a more joyful place to live. Just do what you can. You know what you're capable of today.

Be honest with each other

The older I am, the more I see how people lie, fake or simply are just quiet without saying anything. One day I told myself: 'When I have a boyfriend, I will tell him everything. If I feel I don't love him any more, I'll tell him. If I cheat, I'll tell him. If I don't like something about him, I'll tell him, and I'll expect the same from him.'

I believe honesty attracts harmony. Sometimes, it's so hard to be honest and tell someone how I feel. Most of the time, I find it very awkward to start the conversation about things I don't like or things that drive me crazy, for example when my housemate keeps cleaning the kitchen floor with a tea towel when I told him it's just for drying the dishes (when I'm writing this, I'm laughing because, right now, it seems so funny, but when it happens, I'm fuming), or when I feel it's unfair because someone gets an easier job for the same money I get. Basically, it is important to let the feelings out and be honest, whether it's small things or big things. The weight of honesty is always the same.

Honesty helps me to be in peace with everyone, and therefore with myself. When I am being honest, I don't have to live in lies, I speak the truth, and I share what I stand for. Honesty is literally a definition of nothing but pure truth. Honesty is 'acting now!' and saying what the soul wants to, not what the brain and ego want to. Honesty might be unpleasant, but that feeling of clear conscience is priceless. When I'm facing some unpleasant situation or there is a moment when I need to say the truth, even though the other person might not like it, I always tell myself that moment, that little uncomfortable conversation or awkward look lasts only a few seconds, but can lead to a peaceful state of mind that lasts much longer. From my experience, every time

I was honest and I confessed something I wasn't proud of, or a lie I couldn't carry in myself any more, I might upset people that moment but, firstly, I felt so much lighter and free. Secondly, they always appreciated my honesty. People might not tell you, 'Thank for being honest with me and telling me the truth' immediately, but they will definitely go to sleep thinking of you as a loyal, honest and truthful person.

People are our mirrors and we are their mirrors, so we need to treat them as we want be treated. If we want them to be honest with us, we don't just need to be honest with them, but also to talk about our honesty, and explain to them how important it is that they're honest with us. Then they will be. They'll start telling the truth more often, and also how they feel towards you, because they'll know you are there for the pure truth, not lies, and that your judgement has no chance to attack them.

Communication and sharing how we feel is the key for a smooth and healthy relationship or friendship. In order to be nice to each other, we need to know reasons why we don't feel OK and talk about it. We need to discuss how we feel about a certain situation or towards that person. We need to be honest about our feelings, because that is the way to let our emotions out.

Respect each other

Respecting others is a beautiful quality to have. People will start being more honest and open in front of you; they will know that whatever they do or whoever they are, you won't judge them. I often think how beautiful the world would be if everyone accepted everyone for who they are, respected their needs and acknowledged the unity of humanity and, also, its diversity. I often think how beautiful the world would be if we didn't laugh at each other because of our differences, but admired people who dare to express their individuality and uniqueness in whatever way it might be. I often think how beautiful the world would be if we weren't selfish and blind and respected rights and needs to promote peace and happiness on this planet.

CHAPTER SIXTY-ONE

INDULGE

To indulge means to sacrifice anything to satisfy yourself in the present moment. Whether it's money, time, friends etc.

Now, will it make you happy that moment? Yes! So, go for it. Will it make you happy for the future? I don't know, but do it anyway. Indulging is a very sweet feeling in our lives, usually connected with having some unhealthy dessert, and cheating on the diet we promised to follow. It really does make us happy in that moment. You might say: 'I'm going to buy this luxurious weekend away because I deserve it ' Or: 'I'm going to get this expensive extra virgin olive oil just for this time.'

We can spend money on things that are not necessary but certainly make us happier and our lives more enjoyable in the moment. Indulging doesn't even have to be just about money. We can indulge to be alone, to switch off and spend the whole day by ourselves because we just want a break from humans.

I've been finding happiness in moments when I spoil myself. I love to indulge, love to bring joy and pleasure to my everyday life as often as I can. To me, indulging is a very special occasion (an occasion that can last even two seconds); an above-standard experience I don't do often. I've always had this battle in my head between saving money for the future and spending money spontaneously on things I love. With time, I've realised even when I spend the money on things I thought I shouldn't (for financial reasons, because I had this fear I'd regret spending the money), I did indulge and, guess what, I never missed the money. So, whenever I hesitate over whether to buy myself a treat, I always go for it because it makes my day more pleasurable. It's kind of living the luxurious lifestyle in my head, always going for the better-quality option. I love to spoil myself with healthy, organic groceries, skincare products and cosmetics that are more expensive but make me so happy. Also, it's a great investment for my health and body, so I have two reasons to go for a healthy option rather than eating cheap, usually crappy food.

I love going for the more expensive beddings. Even though it's extra money, I know I love my sleep and I sleep sometimes twelve hours a day, so good-quality sheets will make my night and sleep more comfortable, therefore the whole day will be happier because I'll be feeling good. It can be the Uber ride home, even though I don't have much money in my account, but I'm tired and want to go straight to sleep and know public transport would take an extra forty-five minutes.

I find so much happiness in buying good perfumes, because I'm so sensitive to scents, that I don't care how much it costs, as long as I'm wearing it the whole day feeling amazing. I love high-quality skincare products, make-up, wine, fine-dining, experiences such as going to the concert, tasting local food on my holidays.

You know your financial, personal and social limits, and sometimes it can be very hard, especially if you live from payday to payday. But, if you think you can make your day just a little more enjoyable, luxurious and delightful, always do so; you'll become much happier. It can be anything you were always hesitating to buy or do. Today, do not even think about it! Just do it and enjoy.

CHAPTER SIXTY-TWO

IT IS OK NOT TO BE HAPPY

I really don't want to seem like a person who is happy 24/7, thinking only smiling people can be happy, and that it's necessary to be happy every day, so we can live a happy life.

I want to let you know that there wouldn't be happy moments without sad moments. Without the downs, the struggles, the worries, the depression, the crying and tears. It is absolutely OK to feel down, or however you want to label it, and it is natural and human. The point of my book is to help you find happiness, not to push happiness. Happiness is hidden in moments, and lifetime happiness is hidden in our behaviour, habits, mindset and things we do as people on an everyday basis.

Whenever you feel down, remember it is not a bad thing, and there is nothing wrong with you just because you're not feeling happy. You simply have a reason to feel sad, and you shouldn't change, manipulate or force your feelings. Just because I'm saying how amazing it is to live a happy life doesn't mean you are supposed to be happy all the time.

Whenever you feel sad and you know the reason, be all there; it can last for months or it can last seconds.

I am going through gender dysphoria, and it hit me much harder than anything else before. I wrote most of my book before I became dysphoric but, even when I go through dysphoria and feel anxious and depressed, I am all there and wait until it's over and I can talk with my friends or leave my house again. I know there is always the light at the end of the tunnel.

Basically, whenever you feel unhappy, please don't try to change it anyhow, because you are meant to go through your sad or angry or uncertain parts for a reason. You are allowed to feel the pain, allowed to sit in your sadness and suffering, to feel like a loser. But always know there is not a deadline for such feelings; there is no time frame for our feelings. When it comes it comes, and it comes when we are ready. You know you are going through this experience to learn about you, to grow, find out more about your life on this planet and find YOUR happiness again and carry on your journey to your own 'happy life'.

Be honest to yourself. Be honest to your feelings. Be human.

Thank you so much for reading my very first book.

I really, really hope it helped you in some way, motivated you, inspired you and made you think how you could change your everyday life into an even happier, more blissful experience.

I hope you love yourself and your life more than before.

I hope you believe in yourself and that the universe believes in you as well.

I hope you see love everywhere and in everyone.

I hope you live your best life.

I hope you are (your age) and happy.

Acknowledgements

Thank you to my mum, dad and brother for loving me and supporting me for my whole life. I wrote many chapters because of you, because you showed me what love is and that I could experience it.

My best friend, Chrisen Presence, for being a great teacher, who made me become an even more open-minded and less judgemental person, for always being there for me and for the hours of laughter we've shared.

My friends I met in Sydney who were with me during the beginning of writing this book, who gave me so much love and inspired me and who made my life in Australia beautiful: Jordan Borthwick, Erin Dooley, Siki Daha, Hayley Milano, Kirsten Leo, Angel Garris, Ivanka Matic, Kevin Kaila, Joe Wade, Ryan Englert, Adam Wand and all you amazing shining people I met.

Thank you Michele Rose for introducing me to Daniella's sister; without you the book would still be in my computer.

Thank you Daniella Blechner for being so helpful during the process of editing and publishing.

Thank you editor Lee Dickinson, who helped me to edit the text and adjusted lots of little details I didn't see so this book is very clear and easy to read.

Thank you to Oksana Kosovan for typesetting my book so beautifully.

About the Author

Pavie Valsa is a professional make-up artist and performer who loves to express herself creatively. She was born and raised in Czechia and lived and worked in Australia before choosing to settle in London, UK.

Pavie began her writing career by writing poems, as well as motivating and uplifting quotes, finally leading to the publication of her debut book *Twenties and Happy.* Pavie's mission is to show people how to fall in love with their lives and be happy. She says that she is the happiest person she knows and she loves helping Millennials be the best version of themselves and find their own happiness. Pavie believes in equality for everyone and, as an LGBT+ activist, she is passionate about helping other transgender people gain confidence, power and self-love in their lives.

www.pavievalsa.com
Facebook: @PavieValsa
Instagram: @PavieValsa
Twitter: @PavieValsa

Conscious Dreams

P U B L I S H I N G

Be the author of your own destiny

Find out about our authors, events, services
and how you too can get your book journey started.

Conscious Dreams Publishing

@DreamsConscious

@consciousdreamspublishing

Daniella Blechner

www.consciousdreamspublishing.com

info@consciousdreamspublishing.com

Let's connect